CYC

IN

WEST YORKS

Lanes and by-ways

Derek Purdy

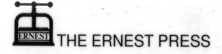 THE ERNEST PRESS

Published by The Ernest Press 1998
© Derek Purdy

ISBN 0 948153 53 9

British Library Cataloguing-in-Publication Data has been registered with the British National Library in Wetherby and is available on request

Typeset from the author's disk by Stanningley Serif
Printed by St Edmundsbury Press

Disclaimer:
Whilst we have made every effort to achieve accuracy in the production of material for use in this guide book, the author, publisher and copyright owners can take no responsibility for: trespass, irresponsible riding, any loss or damage to persons or property suffered as a result of the route descriptions or advice offered in this book.

CONTENTS

iv

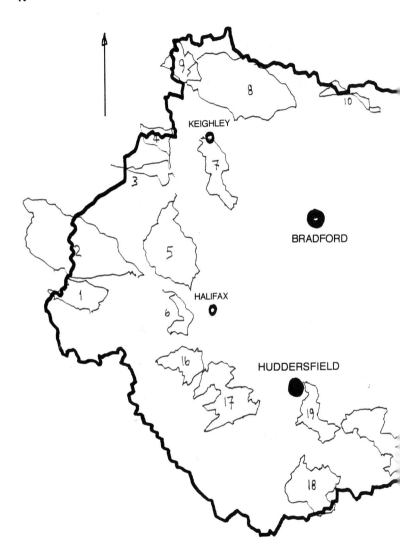

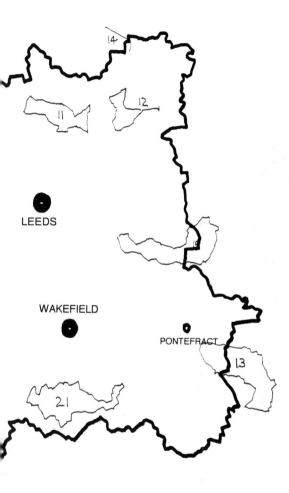

LEEDS

WAKEFIELD

PONTEFRACT

RIDES IN ORDER OF DIFFICULTY

Wetherby Railway	9.5km	Gr 1
Bramham	18.0km	Gr 2
Three Ridings	26.5km	Gr 3
Aireside Powerbase	31.0km	Gr 3
Scarcroft & Eccup	19.5km	Gr 4
The Chevin Challenge	15.0km	Gr 5
Woofa Bank & Hang Goose	16.0km	Gr 5
Ripponden Reservoirs	16.5km	Gr 5
Boulder Clough	16.5km	Gr 5
Haworth & the Hanging Stone	18 0km	Gr 5
Woolley & Wintersett	32.0km	Gr 5
Todmorden Moors	16.5km	Gr 6
Slippery Ford	18.0km	Gr 6
Farnley Circuit	21.5km	Gr 8
Holmfirth & Snittlegate	22.0km	Gr 8
Keighly & Egypt	22.0km	Gr 8
Ilkley Moor	31.5km	Gr 8
Oxenhope & the Windy Moors	28.0km	Gr 9
Heptonstall Moors	37.5km	Gr 9
Emley Moor	35.0km	Gr 10
The Colne Climber	32.0km	Gr 11

NB The distances are rounded off to the nearest half km

INTRODUCTION

At first sight West Yorkshire seems to be full of big towns and cities, possibly not the best place for leisure cycling. Everyone seems to flock to the northern dales, and very agreeable countryside it is, but West Yorkshire has so much to offer. Tourism is on the increase, and rightly so, there is so much to see relating to our industrial heritage, so much worthy of rejuvenation and further use. Much of the ordinary architecture has a unique charm, pure West Riding and all the better for it. I was delighted to see new housing at Hebden Bridge being built in the same terraced style high on the hill as much of the rest of the town, and the sign indicating your arrival bearing a proud picture of the same precipitous streets. West Yorkshire is well worth a visit; if you live there, use this book to delve into the more obscure corners of the county, and you will be richly rewarded.

HOW TO USE THE GUIDE
Much of the biking is not easy; this is tough countryside and you will need a sense of humour to go riding in West Yorks, particularly in the west where there are some fearsome climbs, although you may well be applauded at the top! You will find that each route has basic information, such as distance, the highest point or points reached on the ride - which should give you some idea of the terrain - brief comment on food availability, and a grade. The grades are based roughly on the amount of climbing the ride entails, with of course the same amount of downhilling or freewheeling! But it is the climbs you remember most! I soon realised that overall distance came a poor second to the amount of climbing - you can ride all day if it is flat, but West Yorkshire is far from level. Start with one of the lower grades if you haven't been out for a bit, then aspire to the harder, and more spectacular

challenges - there's some rare stuff at the head of the dales.

A couple of the rides have rough sections, short stretches of off-road, or a short bridleway alternative. They aren't meant to catch anyone out; they usually facilitate an interesting connection, provide an alternative finish or a bit of daft entertainment should the mood take you. For pure off-road riding get Nick Dutton-Taylor's Mountain Bike Guide to West Yorkshire. There are a few rides which sneak over into the other Ridings, and even into Lancashire.

Pubs proliferate. Yorkshire ale is known throughout the land, but do the folks outside of Yorkshire know how much is drunk locally? They would be amazed, but at least it ensures that there is always refreshment at hand for the thirsty cyclist.

BIKES
Mountain bikes are best , mainly because of the state of the side roads, (a malaise not limited to West Yorkshire) but also because of the lower gears. I tried one ride on my racer, which in all fairness is a pure time-trial machine, but ended up walking up most of the Calderdale hills and living in fear of what was happening to my wheels. You will see few other cyclists; many of these hills are too hard for the roadies with their big gears, and the true mountain bikers ride off-road. These rides are something in between.

BIKE PREPARATION
The need for good, well maintained brakes cannot be emphasised too strongly. Many of the downhills are very, very steep and often you will encounter sandstone setts on the hairpins or on the steepest part of the hill. The obvious thing to do is to slow down and pick a good line, but to do this your brakes must be working at their most efficient. Ensure they are!

TYRES
Smooth fat tyres, the fatter the better! or stout touring tyres if you

use a lightweight sports tourer. I found the ideal tyres to be Continental Goliaths 26 X 1.6, smooth in the middle giving plenty of tarmac grip, but with a single line of knobbles on either side which proved invaluable when the leaves fell. At first I thought the old Univega mountain bike looked a bit peculiar with skinny bald tyres, but now I don't even notice it, and the downhill speeds are quite astounding!

WALKING

Don't be afraid to get off and walk on the very steep climbs, and make no mistake, many of these roads are very, very steep. You are supposed to be enjoying it after all. A bit of walking will enable you to climb the harder routes and it doesn't actually take much longer than riding the steepest bits, and certainly doesn't kill you as much.

SINGLE-TRACK ROADS

Single-track roads are not uncommon in West Yorkshire. They don't carry a lot of traffic, but you can guarantee that whatever comes up behind you will want to get past. Self preservation sounds a bit extreme, but many of the car drivers you will meet will be on their limit of ability, so let them overtake you as soon as possible, because they **will** overtake you, whether in safety or not. This practice also shows consideration for the locals who use these minor roads every day, and the likes of the postman who needs to keep to a schedule.

MAPS

Each ride has a sketch map, but this is intended as a visual synopsis of the route, no more. Always carry the appropriate Ordnance Survey map in case you need to take a short cut due to mechanical failure or lack of puff! Landranger 1: 50,000 maps are

the most suitable scale. You need five to cover West Yorkshire.
They are: 103 Blackburn, Burnley & surrounding area
              104 Leeds, Bradford & Harrogate area
              105 York & surrounding area
              110 Sheffield & Huddersfield area
              111 Sheffield & Doncaster area

PLOTTING PLANS

There is a Plotting Plan for each route. This will enable you to transfer the sketch map to the relevant Ordnance Survey map. All O S maps have grid squares superimposed upon them. The sides of the squares are exactly one kilometre, or 1000 metres, regardless of the scale of the map. Every map has an individual number as well as a name, e.g. Landranger 104 Leeds, Bradford & Harrogate area, and also letters relating to the British National Grid, but we don't need these. Our main concern, as far as this guide goes, is to identify specific locations in order to transfer the information given in the Plotting Plan onto the OS map, by means of a six figure reference, which will place the spot at the bottom left of a 100 metre square. Details of how to plot such a reference are given in the key on every Landranger map.

Map references in this guide are given either as : 'Town Centre carpark, Silsden 104/042464', which means you will find the Town Centre carpark, Silsden on Landranger 104, at map reference 042464; or simply 'Woofa Bank 043498'. The latter, which appears more often, will be found in the Plotting Plan list after the map has been identified, in this case 104. If the route crosses from one Landranger to another, as in the case of 'Oxenhope & The Windy Moors', the map change will be notified with the first relevant reference. In some cases the map reference is deliberately slightly 'off' to ensure the correct road is taken.

SAFETY & COMFORT

Conduct on single track roads has been mentioned already, so it goes without saying that a good level of rider competence is an absolute necessity, especially on the hilly routes. If you live in West Yorkshire, you should be a natural! One piece of equipment is a must - the crash helmet. There is no choice, you must protect your head. Buy a good-looking, fashionable, perhaps even colour-coordinated helmet, then you will have no problems wearing it. Some of the cheaper ones are quite functional, but look like children's potties, and no-one wants to be seen looking like that, so these are often discarded and you end up buying a good looker at a later date in any case. Glasses come a close second in the safety stakes; they keep flies, dust, grit and the sun out of your eyes, and may even stop your eyes watering on those big downhills up the dale. A pair of proper padded cycling shorts and padded track mitts will increase your enjoyment considerably. Again, invest in good quality gear, it will provide greater comfort and last longer.

Later additions to your wardrobe can include a good, wicking-base-layer roll neck or T shirt, a warm mid layer with a windproof panel on the front, and even a breathable waterproof outer to repel the rain. You will get away with just about anything in the summer, but bear in mind you don't want to chill too much on the downhills - picture the Tour de France riders stuffing newspapers down the front of their jerseys: they do that to prevent chilling and the risk of catching bronchitis. In an emergency you can always use your map.

ABBREVIATIONS

App.	Approach (from)
Dep.	Depart (to)
E, N, S, W	East, north, south, west
Map ref.	Map reference
SH	Spot height
TL, TR	Turn left, turn right

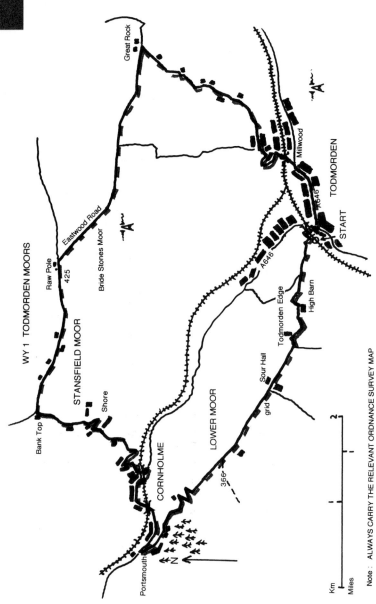

1

Great Rock

TODMORDEN

Millwood

A646

START

WY 1 TODMORDEN MOORS

Eastwood Road

Raw Pole

425

Bride Stones Moor

A646

Todmorden Edge

High Barn

STANSFIELD MOOR

Sour Hall

Shore

grid

Bank Top

CORNHOLME

LOWER MOOR

366°

Portsmouth

N

Km

Miles

Note : ALWAYS CARRY THE RELEVANT ORDNANCE SURVEY MAP

2

1 TODMORDEN MOORS

Total distance:	16.55 km (10.28 miles)
Grade: 6	Total climbing / down-hilling: 447 m (1466 ft.)
High points:	Lower Moor 366 m, Raw Pole, Stansfield Moor 425 m
Map:	O S Landranger 103 Blackburn, Burnley & surrounding area
Facilities:	Full range of facilities in Todmorden; pubs en route at Todmorden Edge, Cornholme and Stansfield Moor

PLOTTING PLAN	App.	Map ref.	Dep
START: Todmorden Rlwy Stn	-	103/935241	NE
Todmorden Edge	E	922244	NW
Portsmouth, A646	SE	898262	SE
Stansfield Moor, via Shore	SSW	915275	ESE
Bride Stones Moor	NW	935270	SE
Great Rock	W	957262	SW
A646, Millwood, Todmorden	NE	944244	SW
FINISH : Todmorden Rlwy Stn	S	935241	-

The grading for such a short route might seem a little heavy, but wait until you have traversed the terrain. If you hate hills don't even attempt this one. Although you can always walk up and free-wheel down, you will need the smallest of your triple chainwheels for much of the route, and the biggest for the other half — there is little in between. This is a true Yorkshire ride demanding Yorkshire humour, Yorkshire grit and above all Yorkshire guts. It killed me!

No wonder so many champion cyclists have come from Yorkshire over the years, the paper rounds in these parts must develop

Olympic athletes. The route looks stiff but fairly inoffensive on the map, then look close at the contours, and the heights attained in so short a distance, up to 366 m (1201 ft.) on Lower Moor, then down to 200 m (656 ft.) in Cornholme and up again, this time to 401 m (1316 ft.) on Stansfield Moor with a climb to Shore that might break your heart.

THE ROUTE

The railway station with its parking facility is signposted from Todmorden town centre. There are other carparks in the town, so merely adjust the ride to your own needs accordingly. Depart downhill from the station, left under the railway and up towards High Barn. Up is the understatement of the day, for this is a most indecent start to any ride. The hill is unbelievable — narrow, twisty in places and always up. Keep to the left at the first T-junction, but still up with a mature beechwood clinging to the hillside on your right. There is some relief at High Barn, but then it is up again between the most substantial stone walls in the county, you may even have time to count the blocks!

Straight on past the 'No Through Road' on the left at Todmorden Edge, then straight on again past Sour Hall, taking care over the kinked cattle grid and out onto Lower Moor with only the wind and the power lines for company. There is a tempting track for the fat tyre brigade in the shape of Bacup Road winding away across the hill to the W — perhaps another day — but once over the summit of the moor it is down, down, down to Portsmouth and A646.

Turn right onto the A646 within sight of the Roebuck Inn, along through Cornholme, then left immediately after the second railway bridge at the Waggon & Horses into a road declared Unsuitable for Heavy Vehicles — another understatement! Keep right, uphill, away from the factory then stick with the main road up to Shore. It is incredibly steep, has a generous helping of hairpin bends and is totally unrelenting. There is a picturesque black and white house near the Cornholme Reservoir, but if you stop you may never get rolling again! There are several little roads and tracks on left and right, but keep heading up, always up.

Eventually, after the longest 1.98 km (1.23 miles) in West Yorkshire, you reach the Bank Top T-junction, where you turn right onto a two-lane road. It looks like a motorway! This high moorland road undulates past the Sportsman's Arms with its dinosaur on the roof, then it is first right into Eastwood Road, but as there is no signpost, aim to pass quite close to the transmission mast.

The enjoyment of a long downhill now starts to register. Ride straight on past the road to the mast, straight on past another road on the right signposted Todmorden and down to the hairpin right at Great Rock. The obelisk you will see on the far side of the valley is Stoodley Pike, a thanksgiving for peace after the Napoleonic wars, raised in 1856, replacing a tower built in 1815 which apparently fell down during the Crimean War, but visible for miles around. The signpost says Todmorden, but watch for it, as the steep approach makes it easy to overshoot. Then it is downhill, given the official gradient of 17% at one point, but surely a lot steeper in the final descent to the A646 at Millwood. All that remains is a very civilised ride along to Todmorden town centre and the final creep back up to the railway station.

High-level recycling. Gatepost protectors fashioned from old
chicken feeders near Todmorden Edge.

Hebden Bridge from the Heptonstall climb.

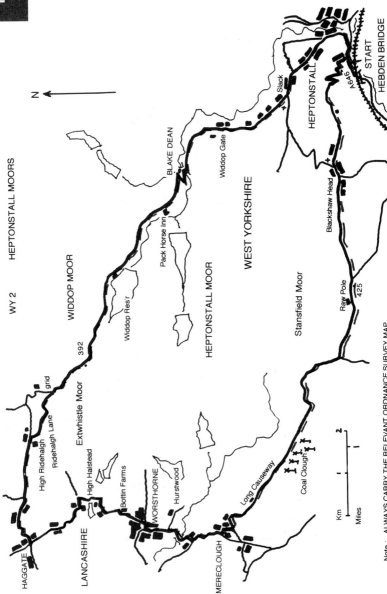

2

N ←

HEPTONSTALL MOORS

WY 2

WIDDOP MOOR

BLAKE DEAN

Pack Horse Inn

Widdop Res'r

392

grid

High Ridehalgh

Ridehalgh Lane

Extwhistle Moor

High Halstead

Bottin Farms

HAGGATE

LANCASHIRE

WORSTHORNE

Hurstwood

MERECLOUGH

Long Causeway

Coal Clough

HEPTONSTALL MOOR

WEST YORKSHIRE

Stansfield Moor

Raw Pole

425

Blackshaw Head

HEPTONSTALL

Slack

Widdop Gate

START

HEBDEN BRIDGE

A646

Km
Miles

2

Note : ALWAYS CARRY THE RELEVANT ORDNANCE SURVEY MAP

2 HEPTONSTALL MOORS

Total distance:	37.55 km (23.40 miles)
Grade: 9	Total climbing / descent: 760m (2493 ft.)
High points:	Extwhistle Moor 392 m, Raw Pole, Stansfield Moor 425 m
Map:	O S Landranger 103 Blackburn, Burnley & surrounding area
Facilities:	Full range of facilities in Hebden Bridge, pubs en route at Heptonstall, Blake Dean, Haggate, Worsthorne, Mereclough, Stansfield Moor, and Blackshaw Head.

PLOTTING PLAN	App.	Map ref.	Dep.
START: Layby A646 nr. Total Garage, Hebden Br.	-	103/982270	NE
Heptonstall	SE	984282	NW
Slack, signpost Widdop	SE	975288	NW
Flask, past Widdop Reservoir	SE	940326	NW
High Ridehalgh, onto Lancashire Cycle Way	S	897351	W
Haggate, Hare & Hounds, Sun Inn	ENE	872353	SE
Bottin Farms	NE	878330	SSW
Mereclough, signpost Blackshaw Head	N	874306	SE
Long Causeway, past the wind farm	NW	900284	SE
Blackshaw Head, fork R at the pub	WSW	959275	ENE
Hebden Bridge, care, steep downhill	NNW	981275	SSE
FINISH: A646 Hebden Bridge	NE	982270	-

Heptonstall was an old hand-weaving centre; then with the coming of the spinning-jenny and its development into the water-frame, small water-powered mills were established on the Hepton Brook. These eventually became bigger mills, powered at first by water then later by steam, and as they were developed the industry gravitated to the dale bottoms, from whence materials could be transported with greater ease, and Hebden (Hepton) Bridge became the larger and more important of the two. Today, as you ride through Heptonstall you return to a village of the past, and it is brilliant. As I toiled up the cobbled street, a bit like an aged waif out of a Hovis advert, someone was playing a piano very well, and the sound filled the thoroughfare. Cycling was nearly abandoned for the pleasure of just sitting on a wall and drinking in the atmosphere.

Hebden Bridge, which lies on the far western edge of what was the textile zone of the West Riding, is unique in the architecture of its houses, clinging to the steep hillside with a toy-like quality, akin to pictures you might see in a children's story book: all it lacks is a castle at the top of the hill.

There is beauty too, some of it very raw like the moors you will cover, some of it like Hardcastle Crags (in fact you will pass above them as you toil up towards Widdop), which is alleged to be the meeting place of exiled Swiss in the West Riding because it reminds them of home, and some of it very modern in the shape of the elegant wind generators swishing away at Coal Clough.

THE ROUTE
Set off NE past the Total garage, over the bridge then first left into a lesser road, signposted Heptonstall. The message is repeated half a mile later by a splendid milestone at a fork in the road high on the hill, but it is still upwards to the former weaving village. Sandstone sets welcome you to Heptonstall — just what you need near the top of a major climb — but this is a beautiful flower-bedecked

village, with a water pump set in an archway near the top of the hill. The primary school sits right at the top of the hill. One can imagine reluctant learners toiling up there in the morning, but it must be a great run back down at the end of the day.

When you reach Slack, Give Way at the main road, and ride straight ahead through the hamlet, then fork right, slightly downhill at the signpost for Widdop. You know you are high when the local fuel merchant is advertising peat as well as coal and logs. After the toil out of the dale, this road seems more down than up, which is strange considering you are climbing out onto Widdop Moor. It all comes to an end shortly after the privately-owned Widdop Gate hostel when you flee down to Blake Dean bridge only to be confronted by the horrendous zigzag climb back up onto the moor. The Pack Horse Inn on the summit might well be a life saver!

The climbing now becomes more exposed but a lot gentler, with Widdop Reservoir occupying the landscape for much of the climb. Then there is a wiggle through a gap, over the col and into Lancashire, but no sign to tell you. There will be few days when the wind will be of any assistance up here. On an overcast September Tuesday the breeze seemed to control the sweltering, but it was debatable whether it was worth it or not. The road now plummets down to the Thursden Brook via the cattle grid and the narrow Ridehalgh Lane to High Ridehalgh, where you turn left at the T-junction, for Haggate. The surface improves but there is a nasty little hill up to the crossroads at Haggate where you turn left into a downhill for Worsthorne via High Halstead. I caught a large ready-mix concrete lorry on the downhill and managed to stay with it all the way to Worsthorne, which did the confidence a power of good, though he was probably the slowest motorised vehicle on the road that day.

Worsthorne can be a little confusing. Stay with the main road signposted Hurstwood, then go straight past the Hurstwood road end half a mile S of the village, then left at the next T-junction, a busy unclassified road signposted Holme Chapel. Turn left again in 0.64 km (0.40 mile) at the pub at Mereclough, signposted Blackshaw Head. There is short downhill, then it is up through the bends past a minor road on the right as you head out onto the Long Causeway. There is a great view of the Coal Clough wind farm as you crest the rise near Causewayhead House. Information boards will give you all the details when you reach the turbines, but the one salient bit of information that impressed me is the fact that "this site enjoys strong wind speeds throughout the year". Hopefully they are tail winds or at very worst coming from the west.

Follow the moorland road all the way to Blackshaw Head, past the rocky outcrop on Stansfield Moor crowned by a toilet bowl, a gesture either made on behalf of rock climbers or to them! Fork right for Hebden Bridge at the pub in Blackshaw Head into the final downhills. The 30 mph speed restriction signs seem to arrive well out of Hebden Bridge, but note them well — thereafter it becomes very interesting to say the least, the road verging on the precipitous. All good stuff. When you reach the A646 turn right along to the Start layby.

The locomotive sheds of the Keighley & Worth Valley Railway at Haworth. Always a scene of activity; always worth a visit.

3

WY 3   HAWORTH & THE HANGING STONE

Note : ALWAYS CARRY THE RELEVANT ORDNANCE SURVEY MAP

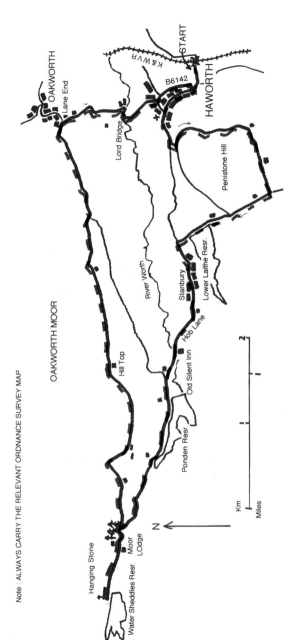

3 HAWORTH & THE HANGING STONE

Total distance:	17.90 km (11.12 miles)
Grade: 5	Total climbing / downhilling: 379 m (1243ft.)
High points:	Penistone Hill, Haworth 301 m; county boundary, Water Sheddles 335 m; Hill Top Farm,Oakworth Moor 326 m
Maps:	O S Landrangers 103 Blackburn, Burnley & surrounding area, 104 Leeds, Bradford & Harrogate area, or OS Outdoor Leisure (1:25,000) 21 South Pennines
Facilities:	Wide selection of tourist-orientated watering holes in Haworth; tea rooms and pub on Oakworth Moor

PLOTTING PLAN	App.	Map ref.	Dep.
START: Belle Isle Road end, Haworth	-	104/034370	W
Dimples Lane, Haworth	ENE	024372	ESE
Penistone Hill, across Lower Laithe Res. dam	SSE	017364	NNW
Hob Lane, Stanbury, to Ponden Reservoir	E	000372	W
Ponden Reservoir	E	103/993373	WNW
Co. boundary, Water Sheddles Res., turn around	ESE	971381	ESE
Hill Top farm, Oakworth Moor	W	000380	E
The Grouse, Oakworth Moor	WSW	104/011382	E
Tim Lane, Lane End, Oakworth	WNW	027385	SSE
Changegate, Haworth	N	030374	SE
FINISH: Belle Isle Rd, Haworth	W	034370	-

Haworth is probably the most famous village in West Yorkshire, a shrine to Brontë worshippers. Maurice Colbeck, in his *Village York-shire* described Haworth as "one of the ugliest Yorkshire villages and one of the most depressing", and you may well agree. As I toiled up the steep, stone-setted main street, I wasn't enamoured with the place either, but my judgment may well have been coloured by the amount of pedalling effort demanded. The stone sets have gaps large enough to accept a high pressure tyre, and the mountain bike was definitely the best option. In 1850 the average life-span in the village was only 28 years; the Brontë family being just over 30. No wonder the place, like the books, has a gloomy air, yet the moorland surroundings are magnificent and we can count ourselves fortunate that we have the time to enjoy them.

But there is another, altogether livelier side to Haworth — the loco sheds of the Keighley & Worth Valley Railway. This is the reason the ride starts at the end of Belle Isle Road, even if you are not a railway buff you must wander onto the bridge for a look at the steam locomotives — they are brilliant.

THE ROUTE

Park considerately in the widest part of Belle Isle Road, which is directly across the river from the K & W V R loco sheds, then depart, steeply uphill to Haworth village centre. You can miss out the old stone-setted main street by sticking to the B6142; they both meet near the Sun Inn at the top of the hill, but really the old main street has got to be done.

Continue W out of the village until you see a signpost for Penistone Hill, but turn hairpin left into the steep Dimples Lane for a clockwise lap of the hill. The views are great, with wind generators all around; the nearest, and seemingly biggest just across the valley at the quarry. When you reach the T-junction on the SW side of Penistone Hill turn right, over the crest, then steeply down to cross the dam of Lower Laithe Reservoir, where they appeared to be installing permanent traffic lights at the time of writing. Once across the dam turn left at the T-junction into a narrowing road through Stanbury, which boasts two pubs, one of which is the Wuthering Heights where one can only hope that the welcome in the bar is much warmer than the bleak sign conveys.

Follow the road NW downhill towards Ponden Reservoir, past the Old Silent Inn and along the upper valley of the River Worth all the way to the Lancashire border at Water Sheddles Reservoir. There is a junction with a road to the right on the steepest part of the climb near Moor Lodge Farm, which you return to for the elevated trip along Oakworth Moor, so you can short-cut the ride a little if you so desire. However the full bleakness and magnificence of the moors isn't revealed until you climb to the county boundary. The Hanging Stone or Water Sheddles Cross lies 200 metres north of the road along the county boundary, but you can't actually see it from the road.

The return ride is a fast downhill — careful you don't overshoot the junction, signposted Oakworth in the bends — then there is a splendid ride around the southern flank of Oakworth Moor for over five kilometres (3 miles), made special on the day with a gentle following wind, and the far fells (the setting for much of Emily Brontë's *Wuthering Heights*) ever changing in the late afternoon light enhanced by the wind-driven storms clouds which seem to haunt this part of the Pennines.

Lane End is the western fringe of Oakworth. As soon as you reach the village look to turn right into Tim Lane, where the nameplate has the rider 'for Haworth'. Then follow this steep and twisty little road down to the River Worth again at Lord Bridge where the road is very narrow and the view around the corners very poor, which is somewhat restricting because the final climb lies ahead and it would have been good to maintain impetus to ease the initial part of the hill. When you reach the crossroads at Howarth, turn left and enjoy the run down the B6142 back to Belle Isle Road, and perhaps another look at the engines.

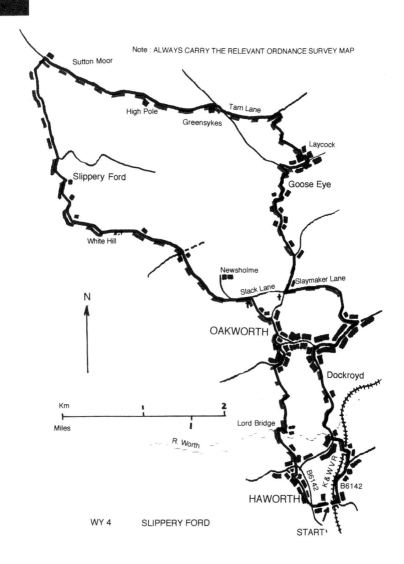

4

Note : ALWAYS CARRY THE RELEVANT ORDNANCE SURVEY MAP

Sutton Moor

High Pole

Tarn Lane

Greensykes

Laycock

Slippery Ford

Goose Eye

White Hill

Newsholme

Slaymaker Lane

Slack Lane

N

OAKWORTH

Dockroyd

Km   2

Miles

Lord Bridge

R. Worth

K & W V R

B6142

HAWORTH   B6142

WY 4   SLIPPERY FORD

START

4 SLIPPERY FORD

Total distance:	17.76 km (11.03 miles)
Grade: 6	Total climbing / downhilling: 433 m (1420ft.)
High points:	White Hill, Newsholme 322 m ; Sutton Moor, N Yorks. 314 m; Tarn Lane 330 m
Maps:	O S Landrangers 103 Blackburn, Burnley & surrounding area, 104 Leeds, Bradford & Harrogate area
Facilities:	All manner of refreshment available in Haworth; pubs en route at Oakworth & Goose Eye; great fish & chip shop within 600 m of the finish.

PLOTTING PLAN	App.	Map ref.	Dep.
START : Belle Isle Road end, Haworth	-	104/034370	W
Changegate / B6142 crossroads, Haworth	S	030374	N
Slack Lane (cemetery), Oakworth	SSE	024394	W
Slippery Ford	S	002406	N
Sutton Moor, N Yorks SP Keighley	SW	103/999422	SE
High Pole Farm	NW	104/006419	SE
Tarn Lane junction	SW	028415	SSE
North Beck, Goose Eye	N	028405	SW
Slaymaker Lane, Branshaw Moor	N	036393	S
Dockroyd	NNW	033384	SSE
Ebor Lane bridge, very narrow	NW	036376	S
FINISH: Belle Isle Rd, Haworth	E	034370	-

This ride is hilly, very hilly, a rider's ride, with a bit of a vengeance. You'll not see many riders en route, a point made quite firmly to me by the only other cyclist I met; one of the local hard men who rides Sutton Moor most days.

The title is a bit of a fraud in view of the fact that there is no ford at Slippery Ford, little in the way of news emanating from Newsholme and no geese to be seen at Goose Eye where even the pub is called after a turkey.

THE ROUTE

The ride starts at the end of Belle Isle Road, within sight of the loco sheds of the Keighley & Worth Valley Railway. Depart W, up a stiff hill into the old part of Haworth, bearing left onto the sandstone sets of the main street, which seems to increase in gradient the higher you climb, then right at the Tourist Information Centre into Changegate. When you reach the crossroads that marks the end of the B6142, head straight across, into Changegate again, signposted Oakworth and down an ever-steepening hill to Lord Bridge over the River Worth. The corners are very tight and the road very narrow in the bottom, then there is a major climb to Lane End, the western fringe of Oakworth.

Turn right at the T-junction at Lane End, down into Oakworth, left into a minor road at the Golden Fleece, T-junction left again at Griffe View, then finally left uphill into Wide Lane, signposted Newsholme. This will take you up over the hill to the cemetery, and a rather fine graveyard it is too.

Turn left into Slack Lane at the cemetery and head W then NW towards Slippery Ford, with Newsholme looking very picturesque on the far side of the little valley. There is a good downhill to the beck below Slippery Ford, no doubt the site of the crossing which gave the farm its name, then another stiff pull up onto the moors and the North Yorkshire boundary. Suddenly the green fields have become white ground, that undulating type of moorland covered with bleached grass, accentuated by a team of cows plodding their way up the fell, arses to the wind, never a good sign as far as the weather goes!

A discreet sign welcomes you to North Yorkshire at the top of the hill, unlike the entries into Lancashire which go largely unmarked, then it is T-junction right at the farm, signposted Keighley, and SE across Sutton Moor and back into the West Riding. This is where I met the local hard man, who did a little loop to have his photo taken, never stopping, then carried on unabated.

When you reach Greensykes Farm, TR into Greensykes Road, but left within 90 metres into Tarn Lane. You will see from the map that you could have gone straight down to Laycock, but the object of this little diversion is to enjoy the manic little Back Lane down into Laycock. Turn right off Tarn Lane after 0.8 km (0.5 mile) and follow your nose down to Laycock, because that is what it amounts to, the shape of the road bearing little resemblance to the map!

Turn right at the T-junction in Laycock, W along to the edge of the village, then hairpin left at Gooseye Brow down an amazingly steep lane to Goose Eye which is narrow, twisty, verging on the precipitous in places, and mossy at the bottom. Great stuff! As you might expect, the climb out of the place is a little killer, but eases considerably over the top, and you should recover by the time you need to turn left into the walled Slaymaker Lane, opposite the cemetery turn.

When you reach the B6143, Keighley Road, in Oakworth, turn right and continue along for 0.76 km (0.47 mile) until you can turn left, downhill into Providence Lane, down past Dockroyd Mill, over the river, then left into the narrow Ebor Lane at the top of the hill. This will take you down over the very narrow river and rail bridge, up onto the B6142, past the chip shop, and engine sheds to the finish. I think something like 'Well done!' will be in order.

A local hard man pressing on across Sutton Moor, just over
the border into North Yorkshire.

Warley Moor in fading light, Press on, there is still three quarters of the route to go.

Ovenden Moor -- first sight of the wind generators as you near the top of the hill.

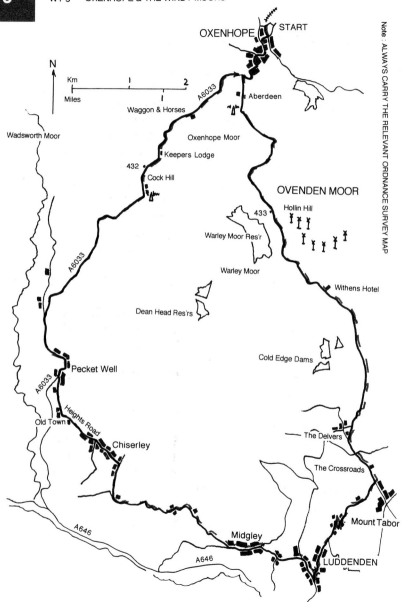

5 OXENHOPE & THE WINDY MOORS

Total distance: 28.05 km (17.42 miles)
Grade: 9   Total climbing / downhilling: 642 m (2106ft.)
High point :   Ovenden Moor, 433 m; Cock Hill
                      Swamp, Hebden Bridge Road 432 m
Maps: O S Landrangers 103 Blackburn,
                      Burnley & surrounding area, 104 Leeds,
                      Bradford & Harrogate area, or the
                      whole route is contained within O S
                      Outdoor Leisure 21 South Pennines
Facilities: Limited food opportunities in
                      Oxenhope, many pubs en route,
                      usually in the most exposed places!

PLOTTING PLAN	App.	Map ref.	Dep.
START: Oxenhope Railway Stn	-	104/032353	S
Aberdeen Farm, A6033	ESE	028345	S
Hollin Hill, Ovenden Moor, 433m	N	035317	S
Mount Tabor, Unsuitable for heavy vehicles	NNW	054271	SSW
Luddenden, very narrow, uphill, hairpin, right turn	N	041259	NW
Chiserley, keep right, hug the moor	SE	003282	NW
Old Town	SE	103/998286	NW
Pecket Well, A6033	S	996293	NNE
Cock Hill Swamp, A6033, 432 m	S	104/010327	NNE
FINISH: Oxenhope Railway Station	S	032353	-

This is the hardest ride in the book in pure climbing terms, or is it? In reality there are only two climbs, but they are monsters. The first, from Oxenhope up onto Ovenden Moor is the steepest, in fact quite horrific to the casual climber. I tried to start easy, up the A6033 from the crossroads in Oxenhope, but it didn't work. As soon as I turned off the main road towards the transmission mast above Aberdeen Farm, the hill on the single-track road bit very, very hard and I was delighted when I could hear a car toiling up the hill behind me so giving the excuse to get off and stand at the side of the road to let him past! When I stopped and turned around I couldn't see the car, such is the gradient, but soon a diesel Fiesta came into view and staggered past.

This is something else to consider — crossing these high moors, particularly on the sometimes rough, single-track road across Ovenden Moor, is obviously the most exciting thing many of the car drivers have ever done; they are right on the limit of their ability, so in the interests of your own safety, give them as wide a berth as possible.

The second major climb enjoys the luxury of being in two parts — Luddenden to Midgley, then Pecket Well to the col at Cock Hill Swamp. Of course there are two major downhills to enjoy and tremendous moorland views throughout. Somehow the ride didn't seem as difficult as some of the others, although getting off and walking definitely helped!

The fatter mountain bike tyres helped again, particularly past the windmills on Ovenden Moor where the unsealed, pot-holed surface reminded me of the Petit St. Bernard Pass between Italy and France. Then down past the infamous Withens Inn where the road has lost much of its tarmac and you shoot down over stone setts, and finally through the villages where the cobble-setted speed humps seem to be specifically designed to wreck lightweight wheels.

THE ROUTE

There is parking for about 100 cars at Oxenhope Railway Station, and it never seems to be full. Hopefully it is that way when you arrive!

Depart S to the main crossroads with the A6033, and turn right up the hill through Oxenhope. Once clear of the village, the main road executes a sharp right turn where you turn left into a single-track road which passes Aberdeen Farm and up to the transmission mast. The road becomes easier beyond the mast, even dropping a bit, then weaves its way up onto Ovenden Moor and the wind farm. There is a rough, pot-holed section before you reach the wind farm information point, which is well worth a visit, but I was amazed to find a huge, 16-wheeled articulated lorry joining the rough from what appears to be a quarry on the E side of the road. I was quickest!

Ovenden Wind Farm is built on land owned by Yorkshire Water and is a joint venture between the water company and Yorkshire Electricity. The turbines are arranged in two arcs to avoid turbulence from neighbouring machines: the generators were made in Denmark, but the towers at Leeds. Generation of electricity starts at wind speeds of 17.6 kph (11 mph) but the average up here is 30.76 kph (19.23 mph), as you may well imagine!

Next landmark is the Withens Hotel, the highest inn in West Yorkshire, always referred to locally as 'The Withens' and infamous for its sporting past, including shooting, cock fighting, and knur and spell* matches. There have been stone sets shining through the tarmac before you reach the Withens but now there is a fair stretch of stony road which cannot be avoided. My mate Paul Eynon says, the quicker you ride over it, the easier it is!

Stay with the main road down past The Delvers, then The Cross-roads, then look to turn right, steeply downhill, before reaching the hamlet of Mount Tabor and into the Luddenden road guarded by a

---

* Knur & spell, also known as 'nipsy', is the poor man's golf.

sign saying Unsuitable for Heavy Goods Vehicles. This is severely downhill, with a tight zigzag which is setted on the inside, all a bit hazardous in the wet. The streets of Luddenden are very narrow and dark, slow down as you enter the village, cross the river bridge then climb gently to the T-junction where you turn hairpin right to start the second climb.

Keep left with the main road at the top of the first part of the hill, then hug the moor all the way to Pecket Well, through Midgley, eventually Chiserley and Old Town along what is mainly called Heights Road, with tremendous views down over Calderdale. The road rises and falls as it hugs the moor, then, when you reach Pecket Well, you turn right onto the A6033 and climb out onto the wild moorland road towards Oxenhope.

This road is very exposed. When I rode, the sun was in danger of sinking behind the far tops of Wadsworth Moor and it had become cold, in spite of the effort. Then as I rounded one of the final bends on Cock Hill, I saw a big, brilliant moon in the E; quite stunning. The Oxenhope stone heralded the top, then it was down past the closed Keeper's Lodge Cafe, down past the open Waggon & Horses, and down into Oxenhope to finish. Some day!

Single-track road up to Delfs with storm clouds gathering over
Crow Hill.

WY 6   BOULDER CLOUGH

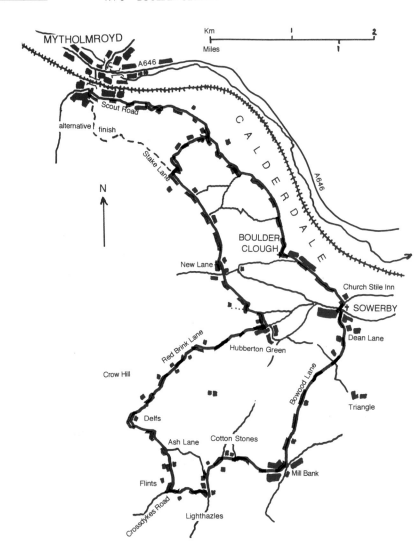

Note : ALWAYS CARRY THE RELEVANT ORDNANCE SURVEY MAP

6 BOULDER CLOUGH

Total distance:	16.79 km (10.43 miles)
Grade: 5	Total climbing / downhilling: 381 m (1245ft.)
High point:	Shaw's Lane Top, Crow Hill 321 m
Map:	O S Landranger 104 Leeds, Bradford & Harrogate area
Facilities:	Pubs and chip shop in Mytholmroyd, pubs also at Sowerby, Cotton Stones and Hubberton Green

PLOTTING PLAN	App.	Map ref.	Dep.
START: Scout Road,			
Mytholmroyd (nr. station)	-	104/012258	ESE
Boulder Clough	N	036238	SE
Triangle	NE	038223	SW
Mill Bank			
(stone sets to junction!)	N	035214	SW
Lighthazles	N	026240	WNW
Delfs			
(not named on Landranger)	SE	016220	NE
Mirey Lane	WSW	033230	NNW
New Lane crossroads	S	028236	N
Stake Lane junction - options	SE	022248	NE
(Grassy option to Mytholmroyd			
via Stake Lane	SE	022248	NW)
FINISH: Scout Road,			
Mytholmroyd	SE	012258	-

You get a lot for your effort from this ride. It says it all about the West Riding. You start in a mill town, Mytholmroyd, and thereafter all the landmarks are either chapels or pubs. It also takes you out onto the high moors on narrow, steep, single- track roads which have a feel all of their own.

For those who don't like hills, and that's a bit hard lines if you live in West Yorkshire, this could be a good introduction. You could walk all the climbs and still get around in an afternoon. In fact you may meet walkers, as some of the route is also used a part of the Calderdale Way.

Boulder Clough, now a tiny hamlet, but boasting one of the most striking chapels in the Riding, claims to be the birthplace of a secret society, and certainly has a quiet air as you ride through, transmitting the aura that there are those here watching you, but in the time honoured Yorkshire way, saying nowt! The brothers of the Henpecked Club met here each Whit Monday, and allegedly still do at another secret location, no doubt due to the cover of the original meeting place having been blown by having too good a time!

THE ROUTE

There is limited parking at the end of Scout Road, some rough parking on the N side of the railway station and across the road at the Shoulder of Mutton if you are a patron.

Set off SE along Scout Road, past the Orchard Business Park, signposted Sowerby. In typical fashion, every terrace of houses in Scout Road has its own name, 'Myrtle Grove' taking my fancy. Then there is a warning near the edge of town, 'Unsuitable for Long Vehicles', and it is. The road climbs steeply; the higher it goes the narrower it becomes; there are many stretches of broken wall; then by the time you ease off to catch your breath you will see that you are well above Calderdale with great views down onto the factories, mills and the Rochdale Canal.

Scout Road becomes Sowerby Lane, then it is straight on past Clunters Lane, Higgin Chamber, and then the outstanding chapel at Boulder Clough. Continue over the most severe of the speed bumps at Clough to the junction at the Church Stile Inn, Sowerby. Turn right, uphill, then left at the church into St. Peter's Avenue and immediately right into Dean Lane, signposted Triangle.

Dean Lane takes you gently downhill past the school, past the big houses, until it becomes Bowood Lane at the junction above Triangle, then uphill again before the ever steepening descent to the T-junction at Mill Bank. Take care on the right fork to the junction — it is very steep and entirely stone sets. Turn right, weave your way through the village over yet more speed bumps, then left into Alma Lane up to the T-junction at the Alma Inn, Cottonstones, where you turn left into Clay Pits Lane, signposted Ripp'den.

Once again you have gained considerable height and it is worth a pause to take in the view. Bear left at the top of the hill into Lighthazles Road at the immaculate bus shelter, then 300 metres later turn hairpin right, uphill, at a black house where a wooden Calderdale Way signpost will confirm the route a short way into the lane. This is a steep little climb, up past Hole Head to the T-junction with Crossdykes Road, and right again around the Flints to skirt the moor.

Eventually you come to Ash Hall Lane, where you bear left to Nook Lane and Delfs, then around the hillside road below Crow Hill into Shaw's Lane. This eventually becomes Red Brink Lane and the reward of a good downhill all the way to the junction with Mirey Lane above Hubberton Green, marked by a board enticing you to the pleasures of The Shepherds Rest.

Mirey Lane, with its well-dressed stonework, will take you N through a series of lefts and rights to New Lane crossroads, where you go straight ahead, then past two roads on the right, one of which is Cat Lane, then to the Stake Lane junction marked by a

Looking back down into Calderdale from Lighthazles Road.

No Through Road sign straight ahead. There is a choice here. The tarmac route turns right, steeply down to Scout Road then left back to Mytholmroyd, or you can use Slack Lane. The second choice involves a fair bit of excitement and a very steep grassy downhill. Go straight ahead, past the No Through Road sign, bear right into Stake Lane which at this point is still tarmac, rough but tarmac nevertheless. Then 0.47 km (0.29 mile) from the initial junction it becomes very grassy, then rutted and grassy, then very steep, rutted and grassy. Follow your nose when you reach the outskirts of Mytholmroyd and you will find yourself within 40 metres of the start in Scout Road and no doubt ready for refreshment at the Shoulder of Mutton or perhaps fish and chips at the junction with the A646.

A pre-war photograph of the moorland track to the Brontë waterfall.

A pre-war photograph of St James Church, Hebden Bridge

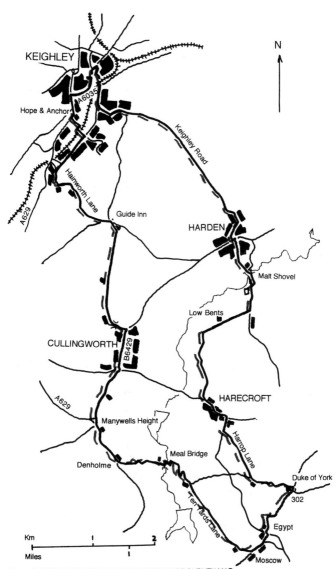

Note : ALWAYS CARRY THE RELEVANT ORDNANCE SURVEY MAP

7 KEIGHLEY & EGYPT!

Total distance:	21.90 km (13.60 miles)
Grade: 8	Total climbing / downhilling: 591 m (1939ft.)
High points:	Guide Inn, Harden Moor (W) 281 m; Moscow, Back Heights 299 m; Duke of York, Dean Lane Head 302 m; Keighley Road, Harden Moor (E) 273 m
Map:	O S Landranger 104 Leeds, Bradford & Harrogate area
Facilities:	There are several pubs on the route and of course, an excellent range of eating establishments in Keighley

PLOTTING PLAN	App.	Map ref.	Dep.
START : Markets carpark traffic lights, Keighley	-	104/061410	SSW
Woodhouse Road, Keighley	N	059403	SE
Hainworth Lane, sandstone sets, steep uphill	NE	056314	S
Guide Inn, Harden Moor	W	065386	SSE
Cullingworth. B6429	NNE	067367	SSW
Manywells Height, A629	N	063355	SSE
Ten Yards Lane	NNW	078346	SSE
Moscow, Back Heights	SW	090336	NE
Duke of York, Dean Lane Head	SW	095345	WNW
Harecroft, B6144	SSW	084356	WNW
Low Bents Farm	SW	084371	NE
Keighley Road, Harden	SSE	083391	NW
A6035, Keighley centre	S	063411	SSW
FINISH: Markets traffic lights, Keighley	NNE	061410	-

Not one for the faint-hearted, in any sense! It is all ups and downs, but the first real 'up' is enough to put anybody off. The lumpy climb over the huge sets of Hainworth Lane deserves a medal if you ride it all the way! If you encountered this in a mountain bike race you would protest!

But what goes up, must come down, and the immediate reward comes in the shape of the arrow-straight downhill to Cullingworth from the Guide Inn. Bear in mind there are bends at the bottom! This first 5 kilometres (3 miles) set the style of the ride which is repeated to a lesser degree thrice more. You really need that Yorkshire sense of humour for this one.

THE ROUTE

There are carparks at the markets near Morrison's or slightly farther back near the church at Church Green where maximum stay is 3 hours, or you can seek alternative space and join the route anywhere on the A629 towards Halifax and adjust the ride accordingly.

The official reference point for the start of the ride is the traffic lights on the A6035, the inner ring road of Keighley, near Morrison's supermarket. Depart SSW and ride around to the traffic light controlled T-junction where you turn left signposted A629 Halifax. After 0.79 km (0.49 mile) turn left after the Hope & Anchor into Woodhouse Road, down over the River Worth, then tight left up over the railway and up to the crossroads where you turn right into Hainworth Road North.

After 1.22 km (0.76 mile) the entertainment starts when you turn left, steeply uphill, onto the sets of Hainworth Lane with the warning that it is Unsuitable for Heavy Vehicles — my meeting with a council lorry inching its way down confirmed this! You may not have time to appreciate it, but this is actually a most attractive stretch of road! Eventually the surface changes to tarmac, you merge left near the top of the hill, and head up to the Guide Inn, so near to town but in a totally different environment.

Turn right in front of the Guide Inn and head straight downhill towards Cullingworth, remembering the bends at the bottom, as you may be exceeding the speed limit as you approach. Turn R again when you reach the B6429 at Cullingworth, through the village, under the railway bridge beyond the roundabout and up Manywells Road to the A629, another stiff climb. When you reach the main road merge left, signposted Halifax, past the Five Flags Hotel, then fork first L in Denholme at a small row of houses into a twisty downhill lane. This will take you down past the pig farm at Meal Bridge then up through tight hairpins into Ten Yards Lane.

The gentle undulations of Ten Yards Lane take you along, and up to the T-junction at Moscow, where you turn left along through the appropriately named Back Heights, and down past the Rock & Heifer (I'm sure I saw that right as I hurtled past!). Then T-junction left and immediate right into Egypt Road and steeply down over the Pitty Beck. Needless to say there is another steep climb up the far side to the highest point on the route, 302 m, the turn at the Duke of York.

Turn left into Old Allen Road at the Duke of York, then right into Harrop Lane, past the big electricity substation, then right again to the B6144 at Harecroft. It is all downhill through Harecroft, so look out for the right turn into a narrow road, guarded by a pair of weight restriction signs. This takes you down, down, down through the Bents to a T-junction where you turn left, down again past the nurseries towards Harden. You can jink left at the nurseries to cut out a bit of the main road, but you will probably be going at the same speed as the motor traffic through the bends down to the bridge at the Malt Shovel where pay back time begins — uphill again.

The climb up to the offset crossroads at the B6429 is sustained but not too bad, but after you turn left and right into Keighley Road the final climb starts to bite The middle section of the hill onto Harden

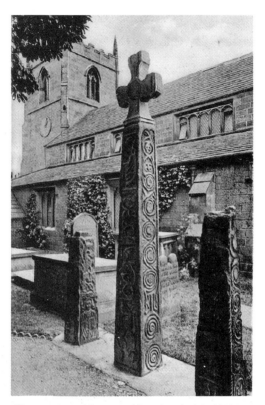

'Saxon crosses' from an old postcard printed by
the Collotype method.

Moor can seem very tough, or is it tiredness creeping in? Once
over the top, it is a splendid finish, downhill all the way to Keighley,
slowing with a view to stopping at Long Lee, but still steeply down,
then under the railway to Keighley town centre, the smell of oriental
spices, and the final T-junction left along to the carpark to finish.

Cow and Calf Rocks, Ilkley Moor.

Ilkley Moor & the White Walls from an old postcard printed by chromolithography (an artist drawing direct onto a stone medium).

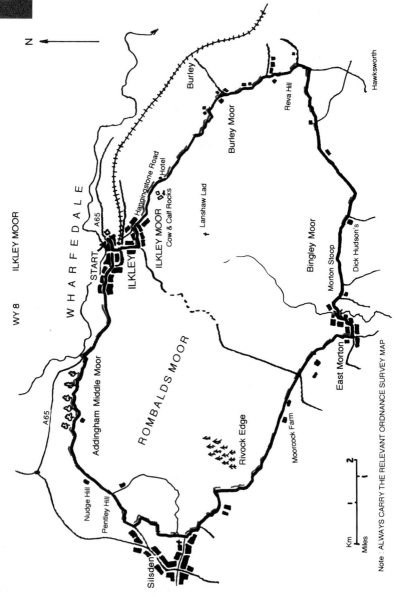

WY 8   ILKLEY MOOR

N ←

WHARFEDALE

A65

START

ILKLEY

Haggingstone Road
Hotel

ILKLEY MOOR
Cow & Calf Rocks

† Lanshaw Lad

Burley

Burley Moor

Reva Hill

Hawksworth

Bingley Moor

Morton Stoop

Dick Hudson's

East Morton

ROMBALDS MOOR

Addingham Middle Moor

A65

Nudge Hill

Pentley Hill

Silsden

Rivock Edge

Moorcock Farm

Km
Miles

2

Note : ALWAYS CARRY THE RELEVANT ORDNANCE SURVEY MAP

8 ILKLEY MOOR

Total distance:	31.64 km (19.65 miles)
Grade: 8	Total climbing / downhill: 574 m (1883 ft.)
High points:	Cow & Calf Hotel 267 m; Morton Stoop, Bingley Moor 275 m; Moorcock Farm, Rivock Edge 281 m; Pentley Hill, Addingham Middle Moor 272 m
Map:	O S Landranger 104 Leeds, Bradford & Harrogate area
Facilities:	Several pubs en route, wide range of accommodation and refreshment in Ilkley

PLOTTING PLAN	App.	Map ref.	Dep.
START: All Saints carpark, A65, Ilkley	-	104/119479	SW
A65, town centre crossroads, Ilkley	E	117477	S
Crossbrook Road, Ilkley	N	117472	E
Cow & Calf Hotel, Ilkley Moor	NNW	134465	SE
Reva Hill junction, SP Bingley	NNE	160430	W
The Fleece, Bingley Moor	SE	124421	NW
East Morton, turn right into Street Lane, SP Silsden	E	097419	N
Holden Gate	SE	066442	NW
Brunthwaite Lane end	S	050462	N
Nudge Hill, Addingham Middle Moor	SW	066486	NE
A65, turn right to Ilkley	SW	092484	SE
FINISH: All Saints carpark, Ilkley	SW	119479	-

No guide of any sort to this area would be complete without the inclusion of Ilkley Moor, so here is a circuit. The roads around the east and south side of the moor carry a fair amount of traffic, so this is not a route for inexperienced riders, especially in view of the gradients involved and the pace one can expect on the big climbs.

Ilkley Moor is actually only a small part of the vast Rombalds Moor which includes several local moors as it stretches about 19 km (12 miles) along the watershed between Airedale and Wharfedale, N of Bradford. On older maps you may find this great sprawling upland called Rombolds Moor, after the fabled Yorkshire giant Rombold, but few will argue that this is the best known moor in Yorkshire, it has encouraged more hikers than all the other moors in the shire and has, of course inspired the famous song 'On Ilkla Moor baht 'at . . .'

THE ROUTE

There is more than one carpark in Ilkley, but the little carpark near Booths Supermarket at the east end of town, next to the old school and opposite the Operatic House on the A65, usually has space, even at the height of summer.

Depart SW along the A65, past Wharfedale Cycles to the traffic lights at Brook Street in the town centre, turn left via the filter lane, signpost Ilkley Moor, then more or less straight ahead into Wells Road, again signposted Ilkley Moor and up the hill as far as the cattle grid. This is as close as you get to Ilkley Moor itself.

Turn left along Crossbrook Road immediately before the cattle grid, past some of the older grand houses of Ilkley, to the T-junction at the grammar school, where you turn right for the big pull all the way to the Cow & Calf Rocks. It is not as steep as Wells Road, but it goes on for much longer! In *Yorkshire Revealed* by C Douglas Bolton, he advises "The most convenient approach to the Cow & Calf Rocks is from the hotel at Moor Top". It is, but we are on bikes and it is a hard grind up Hangingstone Road. The soft ice cream at the Cow & Calf Rocks carpark is just reward!

Allegedly, Druidic rites are associated with the rocks, which bear no resemblance to a cow and calf, but you may see the devotees of rock gymnastics climbing seemingly impossible routes on the biggest face. I am so impressed with the climbers of today — granted the gear has improved, but their athletic prowess is outstanding.

Back to the biking! Beyond the Cow & Calf Hotel there is a little more ascent, then it is mainly down for the next mile or so with Burley-in-Wharfedale on the left, where you will find Iron Row — not alluding to steel or iron workings but to the fact that in the early days of the cotton mills, iron doors were fitted to the mill workers' cottages to protect them from the Luddites. Pay back starts at the Burley junction as you climb around Burley Moor. The road twists and undulates but there is a lot of uphill.

After a further 2.0 km (1.2 miles), turn right, up onto Hawksworth Moor, signposted Bingley, and climb to one of the high points on the ride. Orange Montbretia growing wild at the side of the road reminded me of Western Scotland, as did the breeze that demanded more effort on the brow of the hill. The Scouts use the tiny Reva Reservoir on the left as a sailing school. They should never be short of wind up here. Barely visible below the reservoir lies the little village of Hawksworth, the 'Windyridge' of W Riley's famous novel. It's not just the Brontë sisters who immortalised the area!

Straight on past the road for Eldwick as you skirt the moors in a clockwise direction. Then the signboard for Bingley Moor reminds you of the proximity of Bradford — a bit strange up here, open to the elements — and eventually past The Fleece, better known to the locals as Dick Hudson's, traditionally the starting point for the celebrated walk across Ilkley Moor past the Lanshaw Lad to Ilkley. The only bike route, using the only bridleway across the moor, which is rough and gravelly in places, is accessed beyond East Morton some 5.04 km (3.13 miles) distant.

Stick with this road fringing the moor, steeply down into East Morton where you turn right at the crossroads at the west end of the village, into Street Lane, signposted Silsden. Then straight on a mile later at the crossroads which would take you across the moor to Ilkley.

The plummet down to the edge of Silsden is narrow, bedecked with signs saying **Ice, 17% downhill** - at least! and then **Dead Slow** at the electricity substation near the cemetery, mainly due to the hopeless view around the corner. You will get the idea!

When you reach the cemetery at Silsden, turn right into Hawber Lane, signposted Ilkley. This is the beginning of the final long climb flanking the western end of Rombalds Moor. Hawber Lane becomes Swartha Lane, then after a mile (1.61 km) it meets a T-junction with Brown Bank Here you turn right again, uphill, signposted Ilkley to crest Pentley Hill 272 m, on Addingham Middle Moor after about a mile Then it is down, down for over two miles 3.3 km (2.0 miles). The latter stages of the road become tree lined and occasionally slippery when leaves cover the road, but route finding is no problem — a little white rose nailed to a tree pointing the way to the A65 at the only place where you may wonder which is the right direction.

Turn right for Ilkley when you reach the A65, which is quite busy but a good width. After 2.77 km (1.72 miles) you reach the Brook Street traffic lights in Ilkley, and all that remains is to retrace to the carpark after suitable refreshment.

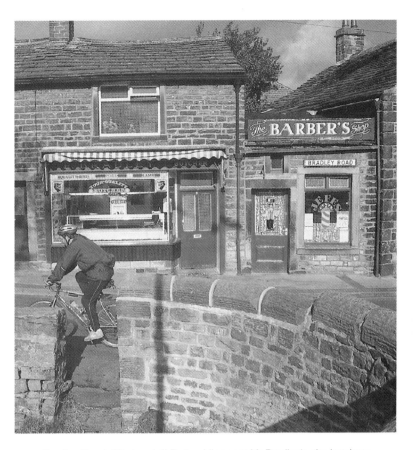

Bradley Road, Silsden. Jeff Rutter riding past Mr Bradley's, the butchers.
The mind boggles if the latter is related to the barber next door.

WY 9   WOOFA BANK & HANG GOOSE

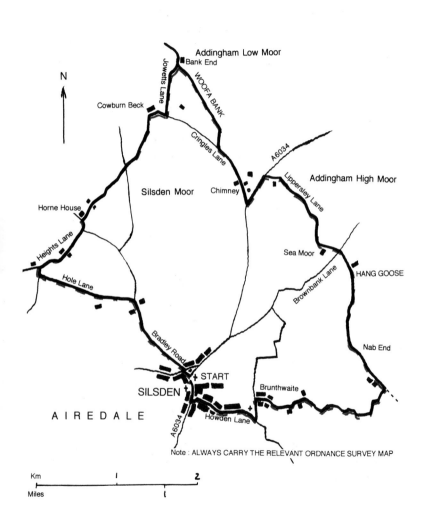

Note : ALWAYS CARRY THE RELEVANT ORDNANCE SURVEY MAP

9 WOOFA BANK & HANG GOOSE

Total distance:	16.18 km (10.05 miles), including 1.59 km (0.99 mile) of rough stuff
Grade: 5	Total climbing / downhilling: 299 m (981ft.)
High points:	Woofa Bank, Addingham Low Moor 292 m; Nab End, near Hang Goose Farm 309 m
Map:	O S Landranger 104 Leeds, Bradford & Harrogate area
Facilities:	Adequate selection of eating places and watering holes in Silsden

PLOTTING PLAN	App.	Map ref.	Dep.
START: Town Centre carpark, Silsden	-	104/042464	NW
Heights Lane junction	SE	023477	NE
Jowetts Lane, Silsden Moor	W	039495	N
Woofa Bank	NW	043498	SE
Lippersley Lane	NW	056484	SE
Brunthwaite Crag	E	060461	W
Howden Lane, Silsden	E	045460	W
FINISH: Town Centre, Silsden	S	042464	-

Simply looking at the map contours surrounding Silsden might, quite justifiably, give the impression that this ride could be horrendously difficult, and I must admit we approached it with some apprehension. However, despite an abominable start up Bradley Road, it turned out to be brilliant. It might have been the fact that it was a lovely October afternoon; it may have been that I had toiled around stiffer routes the week before, but it didn't seem too bad at all. In fact we thoroughly enjoyed it.

Once you gain the heights of the western end of Rombalds Moor which embrace Silsden Moor, Addingham Low Moor and the High version too, the riding undulates but is all quite acceptable, albeit in the lowest gears at times.

In concise terms, the ride has an horrendous start, a great mid section and a fantastic finish, What more do you want?

THE ROUTE

The carpark which provides the Start point is right in the middle of Silsden, between the two churches. Set off NW , using the A6034 for about 40 metres only, then left into Briggate, up to the slightly offset crossroads and straight ahead into Bradley Road, past the barber's shop and Mr. Bradley the Butcher. Initially Bradley Road climbs gently, but the narrower it becomes the steeper it gets.

After 1.22 km (0.76 mile) turn left into Hole Lane. The gradient eases, apart from a nasty little click in the middle, and you are treated to great views of Airedale as you climb. At the top, turn right then right again into the appropriately named Heights Lane, over the top of a rise and down, down on what has been designated the main road, and signposted Draughton. On through the wiggle at Horne House, straight on through a tiny crossroads and down towards Cowburn Beck Farm on a road with low walls and good, all round vision. Just beyond the farm turn left into Jowetts Lane, again signposted Draughton and climb N on a narrow lane towards Bank End Farm, with the rocky outcrop of Woofa Bank on your right. You must turn right before Bank End and ride along the top of Woofa Bank.

When you turn hairpin right the first few metres are a stiff pull, then a bit more serious effort is required to crest Woofa Bank, but the views are terrific, as is the downhill to the junction with Cringles Lane, where you turn left towards the old stone chimney and the junction with the A6034.

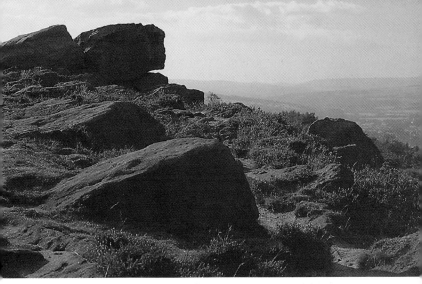

The summit rocks of The Chevin, Otley.

Turn left onto the A6034, then right into the rough-stuff of Lippersley Lane in 0.43 km (0.27 mile). The lane is stony and steep, then quite rutted on the approach to Sea Moor farm, but they make up for that with a pristine stretch of 'Barbour Green' tarmac leading to the junction with Brownbank Lane. The rutted section near the moorland stables is coloured by a surprising and splendid display of cultivated flowers — obviously someone's pride and joy.

After due caution go straight across Brownbank Lane into Light Bank Lane, the last climb of the day, up past Hang Goose Farm, around Nab End, then turn right with the tarmac into the precipitous downhill finish. The gradient triangle says 12%, but that must be the average. Watch out for old duffers near the golf club well down the hill, wiggle through Brunthwaite, then turn left into Hawber Lane and down to the T-junction at Silsden cemetery.

Turn right at the cemetery, then follow Howden Lane all the way to the A6034 in the town centre, where you turn right past the cafe and back to the carpark.

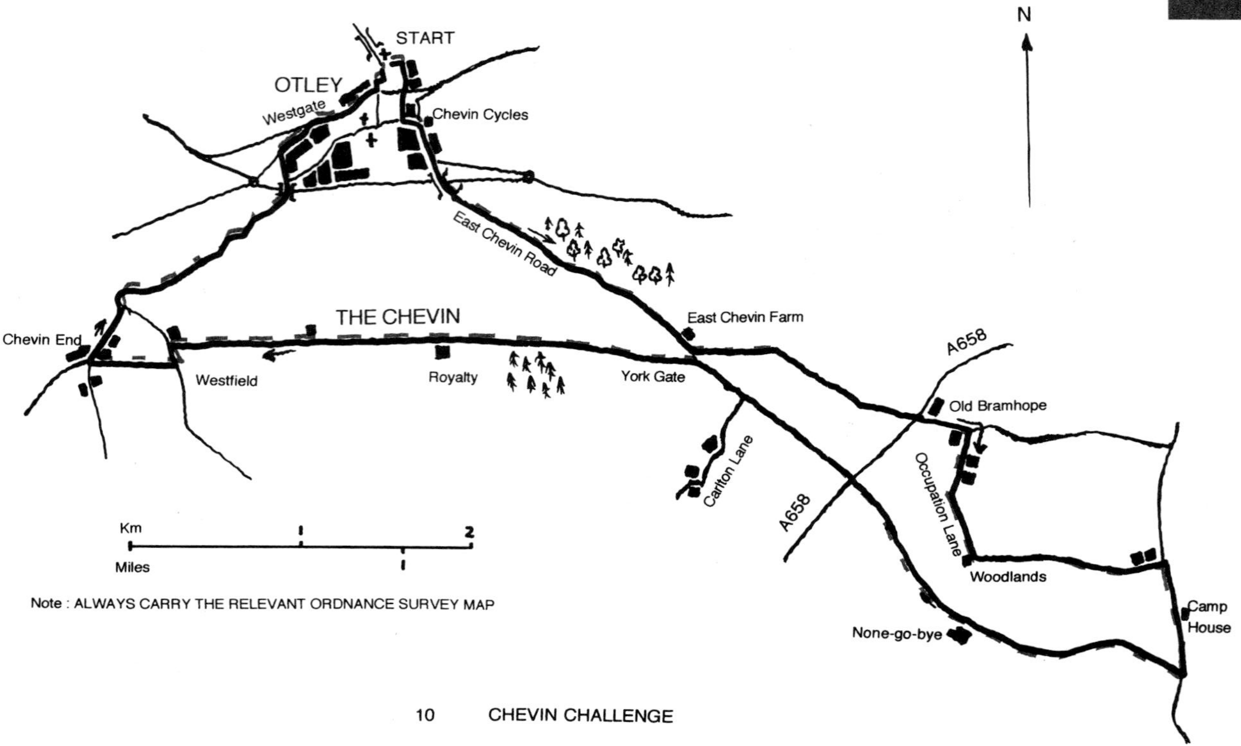

N

START
OTLEY
Westgate
Chevin Cycles
East Chevin Road
THE CHEVIN
Royalty
York Gate
Westfield
Chevin End
East Chevin Farm
Carlton Lane
A658
A658
Old Bramhope
Occupation Lane
Woodlands
None-go-bye
Camp House

Km
Miles
2

Note : ALWAYS CARRY THE RELEVANT ORDNANCE SURVEY MAP

10   CHEVIN CHALLENGE

10 THE CHEVIN CHALLENGE

Total distance:	14.92 km (9.27 miles)
Grade: 5	Total climbing/down-hilling: 305 m (1001 ft.)
High point:	The Chevin road, 600 m W of The Royalty public house, 265 m
Map:	O S Landranger 104 Leeds, Bradford & Harrogate area
Facilities:	Everything you need, including a good cycle shop in Otley, en route refreshment available at The Royalty on The Chevin.

PLOTTING PLAN	App.	Map ref.	Dep.
START: Carpark, Cattle Market Street, Otley	-	104/202457	E
Chevin Cycles (Leeds road)	W	204453	SSE
East Chevin Road	NW	210446	SE
East Chevin Farm	NW	220439	E
Old Bramhope, Occupation Lane	WNW	236433	SSW
Camp House junction	N	248418	NW
A658, care! Signpost Otley	SE	229431	NW
York Gate (The Chevin road)	SE	220438	WNW
Chevin End, The Chevin public house	E	184439	NE
A659, Otley, turn right into Westgate	S	196452	NE
FINISH: Main carpark, Cattle Market Street	W	202457	-

Otley, the metropolis of Wharfedale, is dominated by the escarpment of The Chevin, although dominated might be a bit strong for no doubt there are many folk living in Otley who seldom bother to climb its heights. Chevin is an old British name, a bit of a rarity when you consider our cultural past and the many influences upon it, and Otley is a true mediaeval town, the birthplace of the world famous furniture maker Thomas Chippendale, and a favourite haunt of the artist J M W Turner who did much of his best work here. For a country town it has several old- established industries, but one can only speculate at the effort it took in the days prior to motorised transport to get the goods over the hill to the larger towns and cities to the south. The reality of the problem will manifest itself as soon as you start to climb East Chevin Road!

This is a ride of three parts. The monumental climb to the top of The Chevin, including the little loop down Occupation Lane, the high level run along The Chevin itself, and finally the steep and bumpy descent back to Otley. All will have their devotees, all have something to offer.

THE ROUTE

Depart E from the Cattle Market Street carpark complying with the one-way system. Turn right (S) into North Parade, up to the traffic lights, straight ahead past the bus station, then left, signposted Leeds at the T-junction, past Chevin Cycles and look to bear right into East Chevin Road, which will take you over the ring road via the old railway bridge. This is the first, and most impressive climb, the steepest section rating one arrow on the Landranger, but three in my notes!

The views back over the town provide the ideal excuse to stop on the hill, but some people actually enjoy the climb, which is well in excess of a mile. One rider, who passed me clad in a dress shirt, black socks and black Oxford business shoes, does this every night after work as part of his regular exercise regime. I never found out what he does for a living!

Turn left at the offset crossroads just beyond East Chevin Farm into a lumpy little tarmac road which will take you across to the A658 at Old Bramhope, which can be very busy morning and evening. Take care when crossing the main road, then turn right into Occupation Lane after 0.32 km (0.20 mile). Beyond the houses the road becomes even narrower, steeply downhill with grass growing up the middle, then, after it turns left at Woodlands Farm it develops big undulations. All quite exciting. Turn right when you reach the T-junction, then right again at Camp House junction, marked by a brown sign for a caravan site. The road then climbs relentlessly again over Bramhope Moor past None-go-bye Farm to the A658, then onwards and upwards past Carlton Lane to the Chevin road, York Gate.

York gate is two genuine car widths for the first 200 m then shrinks in and out as it winds virtually due W over The Chevin. Just beyond The Royalty there is a large carpark giving access to the precipitous northern slopes of The Chevin topped by a grand set of rocks, well worth the diversion for what Harry J Scott described as a "hawk's eye view of Otley", and that is exactly what it is.

Continuing W, soon becoming seriously downhill, turn left at the T-junction at Westfield Farm then first right in 150 m and along to Chevin End and the weirdly shaped crossroads at The Chevin pub. Turn right into the final descent, which to be honest, is so bumpy I was pleased to have ridden the route on the Univega mountain bike with front suspension. The road bike would have decreed I slow down I'm sure. Regardless of your steed, you will enjoy the final flee from the heights. When you reach the T-junction in Otley turn right, into Westgate, follow the main road into the town centre, left at the traffic lights then eventually right into the car park to finish.

Otley may have a substantial history, famous sons and an important standing in Wharfedale, but from a cyclist's point of view the most memorable thing is most definitely the ascent and descent of The Chevin.

11

WY 11   SCARCROFT & ECCUP

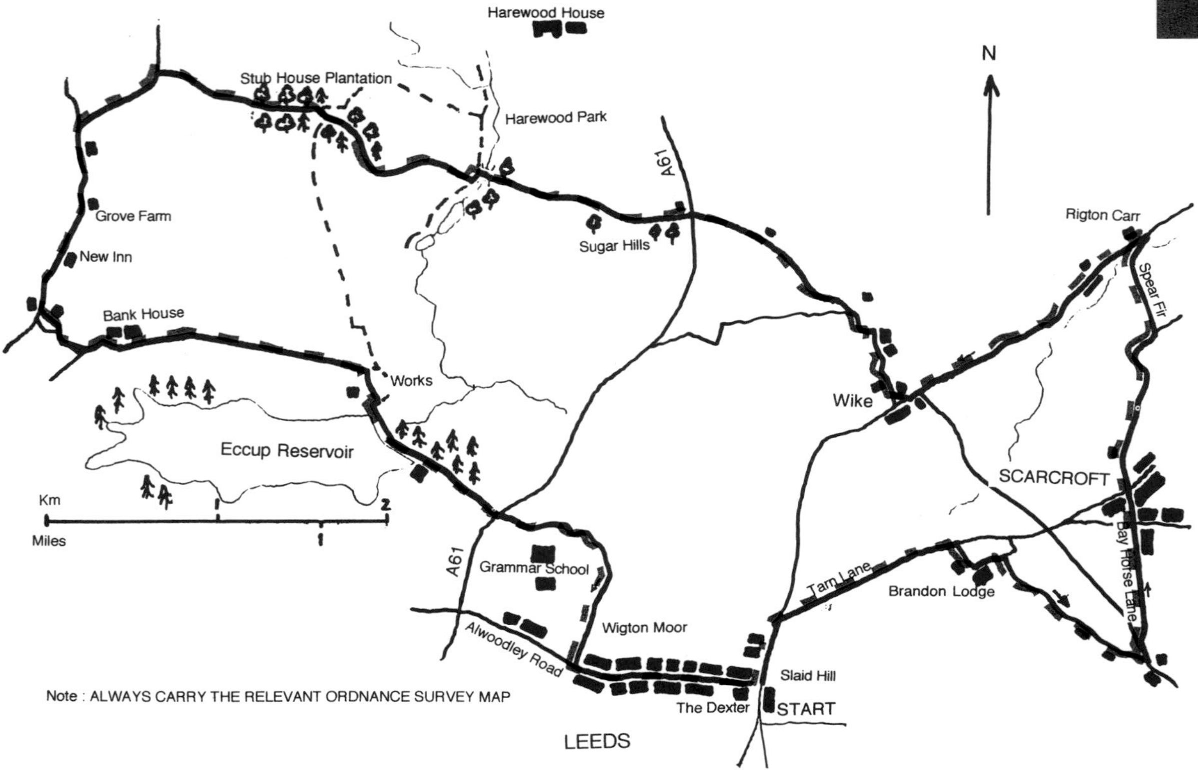

Harewood House

Harewood Park

Sugar Hills

A61

Stub House Plantation

Grove Farm

New Inn

Bank House

Works

Eccup Reservoir

Grammar School

Wigton Moor

Alwoodley Road

A61

LEEDS

The Dexter

Slaid Hill

START

Tarn Lane

Brandon Lodge

SCARCROFT

Bay Horse Lane

Spear Fir

Rigton Carr

Wike

N

Km

Miles

Note : ALWAYS CARRY THE RELEVANT ORDNANCE SURVEY MAP

11 SCARCROFT & ECCUP

Total distance:	19.56 km (12.15 miles), including 3.67 km (2.28 miles) of gravel estate roads
Grade: 4	Total climbing / down-hilling: 262 m (860 ft.)
High points:	Grove Farm, Eccup 151 m; Wigton Moor golf course 152 m
Map:	O S Landranger 104 Leeds, Bradford & Harrogate area
Facilities:	The Dexter at the Start/Finish and New Inn, Eccup

PLOTTING PLAN	App.	Map ref.	Dep.
START: The Dexter, Slaid Hill, Leeds	-	104/329402	NNE
Brandon Lodge, Brandon Crescent	WSW	343410	SSE
Scarcroft crossroads	S	351412	N
Rigton Carr Farm, care at ford on approach	SSW	351430	SW
Low Green Farm, Wike	S	336423	NNW
New Bridge, Harewood Estate	ESE	312434	W
Stub House Plantation, Harewood	E	298438	W
Bank House Farm, Eccup	WNW	291423	ENE
A61, Treatment Works Xroads	NW	314413	SE
FINISH: The Dexter, Slaid Hill	W	329402	-

Any opportunity to ride through Harewood Estate should not be missed, and although this means using a stony bridleway, the rewards more than justify the effort. The estate road in question, running through the park from the A61 along the northern side of the

Sugar Hills, gives a splendid if somewhat distant view of the impressive Harewood House, built in 1760. The park and gardens were laid out under the direction of Capability Brown some time later. This is a very civilised bit of off-road riding.

Eccup Reservoir is a significant wintering site for wildfowl, but also provides feeding and protection for a variety of spring and autumnal passage migrants. You will always find a few mallard, but on a fresh winter day this is the place to be.

THE ROUTE

There is a large carpark at The Dexter and of course it is the ideal place for a shandy at the end of the ride. Depart NNE down the hill from the junction outside the pub, signposted Wike, then turn right into Tarn Lane, signposted Scarcroft. There must be dozens of Tarn Lanes in the West Riding, but on this occasion the tarn is rather elusive, in fact impossible to find! Turn right into Brandon Crescent following the single-track road around past the houses, then right again at a tight corner with what is obviously the most frequently used, but very narrow stretch of the road. There are several nurseries along the lane, but little time to peer over the fence, the layout of the road demands total concentration.

When you reach the junction at Bay Horse Cottage turn left, then right in 60 metres into Bay Horse Lane, signposted Bardsey. This takes you gently uphill past more nurseries, through the big houses on the west side of Scarcroft then down towards a lane bearing the name Spear Fir. Turn left into Spear Fir 100 metres after a right-hand bend, then steeply down to the ford near Rigton Carr Farm. Several substantial potholes on the approach may distract you from the ford, which is bedded with sandstone sets and at times can carry a fair bit of water, so take care. Turn left into Wike Lane at the farm, whose neighbour rejoices in the name *Ponderosa*, the nameplate nearly hidden in the grass at the junction.

There are two right turns into the hamlet of Wike, the second having a signpost saying Harewood — use the first one it cuts off the corner — then weave your way along the undulating road to Harewood Park, crossing the A61 Harrogate Road, to the huge iron gates.

It will be unusual if you don't meet a horse as you ride through the Harewood Estate. Treat them with due respect, as much for your own safety as anything else. The stony bridleway takes you down through three gates to New Bridge, a creative bit of civil engineering, where you turn left for 40 metres then right with the Leeds Country Way, signposted Public Bridleway, uphill on a much smoother track. About 1.2 km (0.75 mile) after the bridge turn go straight ahead at a junction among mature trees, into Stub House Plantation. There are several signposts at a complicated junction with a little triangle of tracks at a lower level on the right, but if you follow your nose gently downhill then out into clearer country you won't go wrong.

When you reach the public road again, turn left up a steep hill, over the top past the New Inn, and then left into a narrow lane that looks like the drive to a house. Now left, left again, and finally left again past Bank House Farm to the Eccup Water Treatment Works approach road. Here substantial speed humps favour the fat tyre brigade. Then, as you approach the filtration site, where at the time of writing there were extensive building works under way, the bridleway has been diverted onto a good, purpose-built track down to the dam. The new track has a quasi-permanent look about it.

We declared lunch at the dam, which went very well until some mangy mongrel ran off with my figs, then it was up to the crossroads at the A61, where the route goes straight across into the narrowest two lane road in the world. This skinny lane, which is a maximum of seven feet wide has been divided into two lanes at the junction — unbelievable. Gravel wash has added to the problem,

Riding the stony bridleway through Harewood Park, with Harewood House in the distance

and it is actually difficult to keep a bicycle in one of the segregations as you attack the hill.

This final bumpy lane takes you around the back of the very impressive, new Leeds Grammar School, through the golf course at Wigton Moor where there are warnings of flying golf balls, then out onto Alwoodley Road where you turn left, and back to The Dexter.

The ancient milestone at the triangular Milner Lane/Thorner Lane junction, north of Thorner. This is on the Roman road to York, but there is debate regarding the age of the stone.

12

WY 12   BRAMHAM

Note : ALWAYS CARRY THE RELEVANT ORDNANCE SURVEY MAP

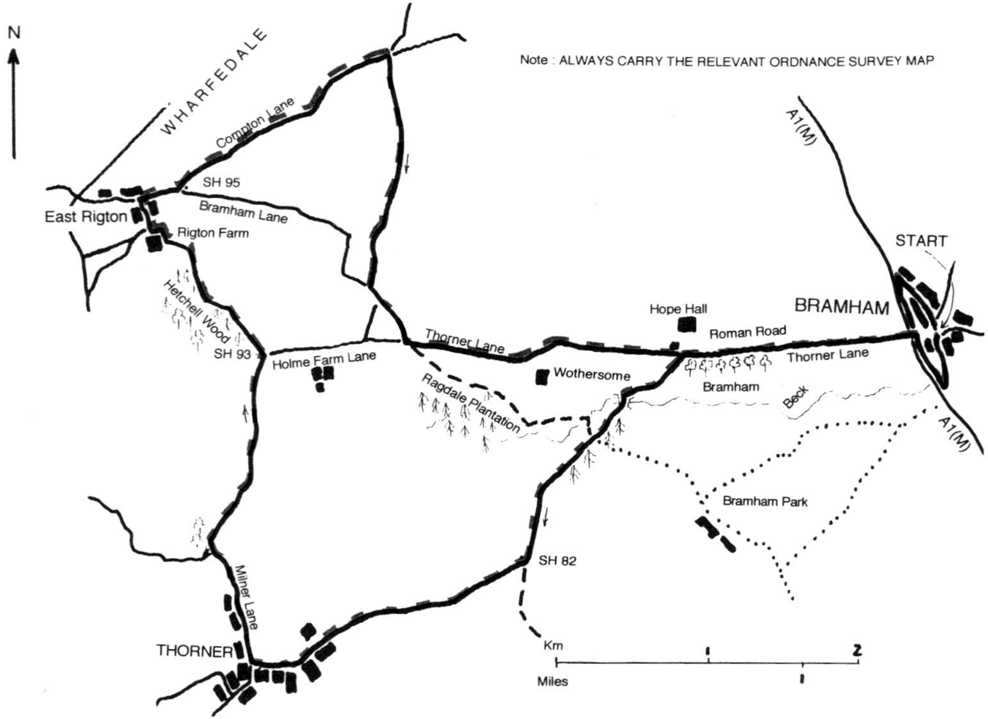

A1(M)

START

BRAMHAM

A1(M)

Thorner Lane

Roman Road

Hope Hall

Bramham

Bramham Park

Wothersome

SH 82

Thorner Lane

Ragdale Plantation

Holme Farm Lane

WHARFEDALE

Compton Lane

SH 95

Bramham Lane

Rigton Farm

Hetchell Wood

SH 93

Milner Lane

East Rigton

THORNER

Km

Miles

N

N

12 BRAMHAM

Total distance:	18.31 km (11.37 miles)
Grade: 2	Total climbing/downhilling: 135 m (443ft.)
High point:	Compton Lane, East Rigton, 100 m
Maps:	O S Landrangers 104 Leeds, Bradford & Harrogate, 105 York & surrounding area.
Facilities:	Red Lion and White Horse pubs in Bramham, also pub in Thorner.

PLOTTING PLAN	App.	Map ref.	Dep.
START: Bramham village	-	105/425429	S
A1(M) bridge, Bramham	SSE	423428	W
Hope Hall junction, SH 66	E	408427	SW
SH 82	N	104/397413	SW
Thorner, Milner Lane	E	379406	N
SH 93 near Hetchell Wood	SSW	380428	NW
East Rigton, Compton Lane, SH 95	WSW	374431	NE
Compton crossroads	SW	388448	S
Crossroads, Thorner Lane (one white bridleway)	NNW	389429	E
Hope Hall junction, SH 66	W	105/408427	E
A1(M) bridge, Bramham	W	423428	N
FINISH: Bramham village	NW	425429	-

This is one of the most accessible rides in the guide, the village of Bramham lying on the A1 Great North Road about 6 km (4 miles) south of Wetherby. The route toddles SW to the quiet village of Thorner, then describes a big arc N, then E along the elevated southern flanks of Wharfedale, affording great views over the rich farmlands towards Harrogate, North Yorkshire, and beyond.

Bramham has suffered greatly at the hands of the A1 road, and nowadays is easy to miss as you hurtle past on the new three-lane motorway. Even the entrance to Bramham Park has been relocated to accommodate the widening of the Great North Road, and some of the village allotments have been severed from their tenants by several hundred metres. Once a handy stopping place for through travellers, you now need to make a special effort to visit the village, but you will still find all the amenities within 100 metres of the A1.

THE RIDE

Start at the war memorial near the Red Lion and head S on the old A1, signposted The North, The South, Doncaster. This will take you gently uphill to a T-junction, where you turn right, signposted The North, Bramham Park; then left across the new bridge over the A1(M) and west along the Roman Road towards Thorner. As you climb towards the bridge, take note of the conifers planted along the east side of the road to shield Bramham from the noise and fumes of the A1; then at the far side of the bridge you will see the defiant allotments on your right, one of which flew the Union Jack at half mast in tribute to Diana, Princess of Wales, who had died tragically only three days earlier.

The old Roman Road now bears the name Thorner Lane, but this was part of the cross-country route from the Ribble estuary through Olicana (Ilkley) to Calcaria (Tadcaster) and on to Ebvracvm (York), an important trade route in Roman times.

The straight, leafy carriageway runs more or less due W to the fork at Hope Hall junction, where you turn left, past the site of the mediaeval village of Wothersome, down over Bramham Beck, then past the new, visitors' entrance to Bramham Park and on to Thorner.

(I can never pass Bramham Park without a smile. In February 1979 I was navigating John Lindores in a 'full house' Ford Escort RS 2000 on the Mintex International Rally, which included a special stage through Bramham Park, timed to the second. A generous amount of snow had fallen and high speed motoring was exciting to say the least. John was the current North of England Autocross champion at the time, and an artist at driving sideways. As we passed behind the beautiful Queen Anne Mansion, the course turned sharp right to follow the main drive down through the park, and John gave the car the boot, which as anticipated threw it sideways in a great shower of snow but it accelerated faster than anyone else because earlier competitors had by this time polished the normal surface. It was brilliant, John continuing totally unabated as the car slid from side to side, with the crowd cheering, the commentator going ballistic, and an important Police inspector who had positioned himself between the drive and the crowd trying to look unmoved by the exhibition. The faster we went, the more dramatic the skids, but the inspector stood his ground, until at last he forgot his importance and turned to run. You can imagine it, the crowd were on their feet, we were doing about 70 mph sideways through the snow, and the inspector was getting more wheelspin than us in his ignominious attempts at escape. I couldn't call the instructions for laughing and we had motor sport enthusiasts ringing recalling the incident for years after. Heady days!)

Back to the cycling. When you reach Thorner, turn right into Milner Lane at the T-junction at the bottom of the hill. The Unsuitable for long vehicles sign will give you an inkling of what lies ahead. There is a bumpy climb to a triangular road junction where Milner Lane bears right past a huge old milestone, signposted East Rigton, then a similar bearing left into Holme Farm Lane, which will take you all the way, eventually, to East Rigton, but take care in the S-bends near Rigton Farm.

At East Rigton turn right into Rigton Green, signposted East Keswick, then bear left into the very narrow Compton Lane which will take you, high above Wharfedale, to Compton crossroads where you turn S to complete the loop. Take care on the downhill approach to the crossroads, because you need to turn sharp right uphill, and at the time of writing the fingerpost was broken.

There is fairly gentle ride back through the fields to Bramham Lane, where you bear left at the tiny junction, then left again at the triangle at the top of the rise to take you SE to the crossroads at Thorner Lane. One of the arms of the crossroads is a broad bridleway down through Ragdale Plantation and E to Bramham Park which might be a temptation for those with fatter tyres, but the official route turns due E to follow the old Roman Road back to Bramham. Take care in the dip beyond the entrance to Wothersome Farm, as gravel often accumulates in the bottom after rain. Then it is straight on to re-cross the A1(M), left with 'Local traffic only' and around into Bramham to finish.

A satanic-looking Eggborough at only 1300 hrs on a still but .
freezing December day.

13

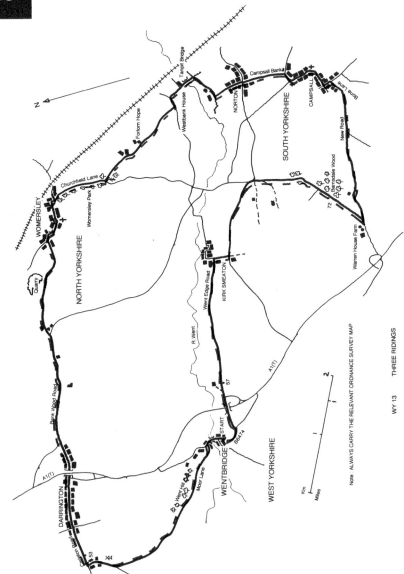

N

Tanpit Bridge

Campsall Bank

Forlorn Hope

Westbank House

NORTON

CAMPSALL

Bond Lane

SOUTH YORKSHIRE

New Road

Churchfield Lane

WOMERSLEY

Womersley Park

NORTH YORKSHIRE

Barnsdale Wood

72

Quarry

Warren House Farm

R. Went

Went Edge Road

KIRK SMEATON

57

A1(T)

Bank Wood Road

START

B6474

A1(T)

WENTBRIDGE

WEST YORKSHIRE

Moor Lane

DARRINGTON

Went Hill

Cridling Stubbs

53

Km

Miles

1

2

Note   ALWAYS CARRY THE RELEVANT ORDNANCE SURVEY MAP

WY 13   THREE RIDINGS

13 THREE RIDINGS

Total distance:	26.64 km (17.17 miles)
Grade: 3	Total climbing/downhilling: 191 m (627ft.)
High point:	Barnsdale Wood 72 m
Maps:	O S Landranger 111 Sheffield & Doncaster area, and a very short stretch on 105 York, where the sketch map will suffice.
Facilities:	Pubs and restaurants in Wentbridge, other pubs en route.

PLOTTING PLAN	App.	Map ref.	Dep.
START: Blue Bell Inn, Wentbridge, B6474	-	111/488171	NNE
Went Hill, head for the topless windmill	SSE	472188	N
Carleton Road, SH 53, through Darrington	WSW	105/475201	ENE
Darrington, E under A1(T), into N Yorks	WNW	111/489199	E
Womersley Quarry, down into Womersley	WNW	523194	SE
Churchfield Lane, Womersley	NNW	536187	S
Tanpit Bridge, into S Yorks	NNW	548162	SSE
Campsall Bank, Norton	N	545162	S
Bone Lane, Campsall	E	540136	SW
Barnsdale Wood, 72 m	SW	522142	NE
Kirk Smeaton, SH 35, signpost Kirk Smeaton	ESE	517163	N
Went Edge Road, Trig. pt. 57	E	507168	W
FINISH: Wentbridge, B6474	SW	488171	-

Three Ridings is a complete misnomer: a more honest title for this ride would be 'Three of the modern administrative districts of Yorkshire', which simply doesn't have the same ring to it. In truth the entire ride is contained within the old West Riding, which extended as far east as Drax and Goole, according to Moule's map of 1830. The cooling towers of Drax power station can be seen well to the east from Womersley, which lies in the modern North Yorks, and when you cross the tiny Tanpit Bridge into South Yorkshire, and perhaps be somewhat surprised to find yourself in the Metropolitan Borough of Doncaster this far north, bear in mind that both Sheffield and Doncaster lay in the old West Riding.

The ride starts at Wentbridge, which sits, or sat on the Great North Road, long before it became the A1. The *British Road Book, volume III (1897)* of the Cyclists' Touring Club quotes "Steep descent to Wentbridge, requiring care; cross river, and ascend long hill, after which a fairly level run to Ferrybridge. Indifferent surface." There is room to park on the wide bridge over the River Went, or up at the Blue Bell if you intend to patronise the establishment. The village is quiet now, well removed from the A1 trunk road, but it has had its moments, one of the more picturesque being the regular collection of the pupils of Ackworth Quaker School by a cart drawn by the school bull, in the eighteenth century.

You don't "ascend the long hill" described in the British Road Book, but dive off left immediately north of the bridge and take a more leisurely climb to Darrington, with its white church built of magnesium limestone, then east to Womersley past the old limestone quarry. The village, mentioned in the Domesday Book, which would not look out of place in the Cotswolds with its mellow stonework, has another imposing church, an Elizabethan hall and an old moated farm, most of which are hidden from view by the estate wall as you wiggle along the main street.

The rolling countryside is a complete contrast to the Pennine fringes at the western end of the county, easier to ride, with a high point of only 72 m at Barnsdale Wood, but with some interesting and extensive views for all that — in fact some impressive panoramas, usually dominated by the four major power stations.

THE ROUTE
Ride north across the bridge over the River Went, then turn left into Moor Lane (a mainly unfenced road around the base of the wooded Went Hill) past the motorcycle scrambles course, or is it a quad track, and through the turnip fields which provided a strangely reassuring and unique aroma on a cold December morning.

Eventually you pass a beheaded windmill and arrive at a T-junction, Carleton Road, where you turn right, signpost Darrington. Follow this E through Darrington, under the A1(T) into Bank Wood Road and gently down into North Yorkshire, where the leafless trees which lined the road still seemed to give some protection from the frosty morning.

The gentle climb takes you up to and along a raised plateau, past the old Womersley quarry, glinting cream but not over warm in the wintry sun, then down and through the village with peeks into courtyards, and straight on into Churchfield Lane, signposted Smeaton at a tight left bend, and S up the eastern side of Womersley Park.

Fork left, signpost Walden Stubbs in the midst of the flat fields, wiggle past the first farm, then the second, bearing the name Forlorn Hope, which was for sale at the time of writing! The next T-junction has a brace of signposts, turn left towards Norton then right within 100 metres with the main road, past Westbank House and over the humped Tanpit Bridge into South Yorkshire. Follow the tarmac all the way into Norton, then jink right and left towards Campsall at the Royal Oak.

When you reach Campsall turn right, follow the main road down through the village, eventually turning right into Bone Lane, which becomes New Road and heads west all the way to Warren House Farm. Here you turn right to Barnsdale Wood, signposted Norton, Smeaton and the highest point on the ride. The wood leads into the best downhill of the day and a complicated junction where you 'Give Way', then turn left downhill towards Kirk Smeaton, but there is no signpost for us.

The crossroads to the S of Kirk Smeaton have a fine, old sign- post which points you right into the village. Then look for the first left into Went Edge Road which climbs up through open fields, past a large container depot in the middle of the countryside, but within a stone's throw of the A1, over the trunk road, then right and down that "Steep descent to Wentbridge, requiring care", to finish.

Kingbarrow Bridge, Wetherby. The end of the leafy tunnel through the cutting.

Railway Inn, Spofforth. A good sign, good beer and good food.

WETHERBY RAILWAY - THE HARLAND WAY

WY 14

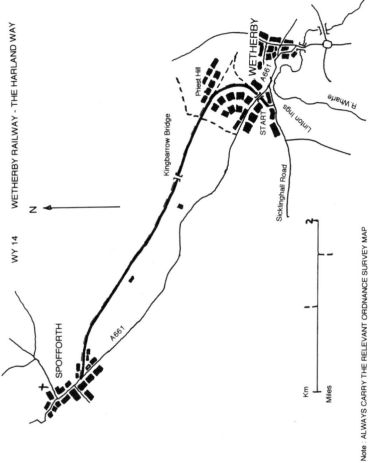

N

SPOFFORTH

A661

Kingbarrow Bridge

Priest Hill

WETHERBY

A661

START

Linton Ings

R.Wharfe

Sicklinghall Road

Km

Miles

Note : ALWAYS CARRY THE RELEVANT ORDNANCE SURVEY MAP

14 WETHERBY RAILWAY - THE HARLAND WAY

Total distance:	9.52 km (5.92 miles)
Grade: 1	Total climbing/downhilling: 15 m (49 ft.)
High point:	Kingbarrow Bridge, 50 m
Maps:	O S Landranger 104 Leeds, Bradford & Harrogate area
Facilities:	Pubs, restaurants and take-aways in Wetherby, Railway Hotel (all day food) at Spofforth.

PLOTTING PLAN	App.	Map ref.	Dep.
START: Carpark off Sicklinghall Road, Wetherby	-	104/397483	ENE
Priest Hill junction	SSE	398491	NW
Cycle Route, Wetherby - Spofforth	SE	381500	NW
Spofforth, Railway Hotel. Turn around and retrace	E	366507	E
Kingbarrow Bridge (ride underneath!)	WNW	389495	ESE
Priest Hill junction	NW	398491	SSE
FINISH: Sicklinghall Road carpark	ENE	397483	-

The old railway line from Wetherby to Spofforth has been converted to a shared facility for both cyclists and pedestrians. In other words a railway path, of which there are several dotted around the country — excellent traffic-free avenues suitable for even the youngest or most nervous rider, whilst at the same time providing a most relaxing ride for anyone. You regularly find serious cyclists using this route to miss out a busy stretch of the A661. The easiest ride in the guide, but worth a hurl at any time of year.

Parking near the start of the ride used to be a problem, inevitably entailing an awkward ride through the narrow streets of Wetherby — not good if there were youngsters in the party — but the creation of a new, large carpark off Sicklinghall Road, which hugs the river on the west side of town, has completely eradicated the problem, and you can now ride straight onto the railway path without encountering motorised traffic at all.

Additional work on the track surface has also been carried out, and whilst this is technically an off-road route the surface is now good enough for the skinniest of wheels, although at the time of writing the carpark is pebbly.

Initially I intended this to be part of a circular tour, but after enjoying the quiet of the railway path, decided that a traffic free out-and-back ride gave the most pleasure.

THE ROUTE

The carpark is signposted off Sicklinghall Road, which in turn is an offshoot of the A661, Harrogate road, on the western side of Wetherby, above the river at Linton Ings. A blue Cycleway sign saying Spofforth guides you in.

Depart NE along the old railway, under the A661, then swing left into a substantial cutting. Quite a dramatic start. After 0.85 km (0.53 mile) swing left again where the old lines merge near Priest Hill. Another 450 metres takes you straight ahead, through a double set of barriers, where a bridleway crosses the line, and you are firmly committed to the route.

Another deepening cutting leads to Kingbarrow Bridge, which looks strangely like the end of a tunnel, especially at the height of summer when the trees are in full leaf. Soon after the bridge you burst out into open country and a splendid run along to Spofforth, a total distance for the outward leg of 4.76 km (2.96 miles).

Huge RJB (R J Budge Mining) draglines at the opencast site
between Swillington and Allerton Bywater.

The railway path now terminates at a new housing estate where
the street will take you around to the A661 where you turn left along
to the Railway Hotel, but if there are youngsters in the party it will
be a lot safer to keep straight on with the route of the old railway, on
a muddy little path which will take you to the beer garden within
100 metres.

The return route is simply a reversal of the outbound ride, and
just as good, but don't forget to swing right when you get to Priest
Hill or you could end up in completely the wrong part of Wetherby!

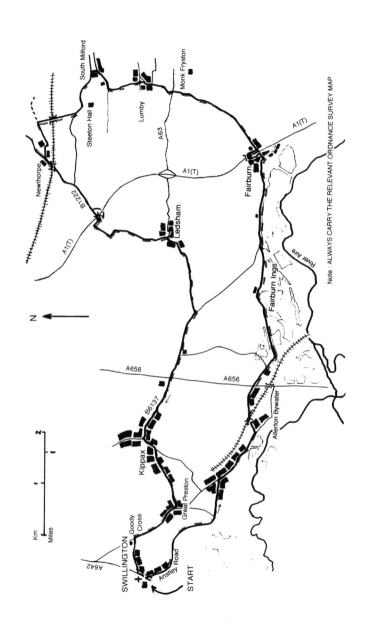

WY 15   AIRESIDE POWERBASE

N

Km
Miles

South Milford

Steeton Hall

Newthorpe

B1222

A1(T)

Lumby

Monk Fryston

A63

A1(T)

A1(T)

Ledsham

Fairburn

River Aire

Fairburn Ings

A656

A656

B6137

Allerton Bywater

Kippax

Great Preston

Goody Cross

SWILLINGTON

A642

Anstley Road

START

Note : ALWAYS CARRY THE RELEVANT ORDNANCE SURVEY MAP

15 AIRESIDE POWERBASE

Total distance:	30.85 km (19.16 miles)
Grade: 3	Total climbing/downhilling: 202 m (663ft.)
High point:	B6137 Kippax 74 m
Maps:	O S Landrangers 104 Leeds, Bradford & Harrogate area, 105 York & surrounding area
Facilities:	Pub grub at the Start/Finish, Allerton Bywater, Fairburn, Ledsham, Kippax. You will not starve!

PLOTTING PLAN	App.	Map ref.	Dep.
START: The Swillington A642		104/383303	NE
Anstley Road, Swillington	NNW	397290	SSE
Great Preston	WNW	105/407286	SSE
A656 Crossroads	NW	426280	SE
Fairburn Ings	W	460279	E
Fairburn, loop over bridge over A1(T)	SW	472279	NE
A63, Monk Fryston, care	S	484297	N
Steeton Hall, South Milford	ESE	485315	W
B1222 Newthorpe	E	471323	SW
Under A1(T) on B1222	NE	460312	NW
Ledsham	N	455297	SSW
A656, care, crossroads onto B6137	ESE	428297	WNW
Kippax	NE	313300	W
Great Preston	E	401296	NNW
Goody Cross	SE	104/394305	W
Swillington, A642	E	385305	SW
FINISH: The Swillington	NE	383303	

Twenty years ago this ride would have been a mining tour, the villages in this extreme easterly region of West Yorkshire all surrounding at least one pit. Today the only obvious reminder of the coalfields might be the huge RJB draglines at the edge of the opencast workings between Swillington and Allerton Bywater, but if you look closely, or come from a mining background there are signs galore. Landscaped pitheaps, pit ponds or ings in local parlance, defunct railways, and the cloudy cooling towers of Ferrybridge power station, enormous monuments to the age when coal was king.

The route includes a cheeky foray across the Great North Road into N Yorkshire, mainly because there wasn't a convenient loop without doing this, but as soon as you cross the A1(T) you will notice a change in the countryside, hedgeless fields being the most obvious sign. See what you think.

Along the River Aire, be it in its natural form or in the canalised version, there are numerous Ings. This derives from the Norse or Danish when it meant a meadow, but those adjacent to the Aire are ponds, some created as pits, some as reservoirs or canal basins, but many due to subsidence as a result of coal extraction. There were always pit ponds which attracted wildlife; in fact the pitmen often had an outstanding knowledge of wild birds, long before birdwatching became popular, and it was a privilege as a youngster to be introduced to their secrets, "but only if you behaved yourself!"

THE ROUTE
Parking is very limited in Swillington. There is usually room at the pub, The Swillington, so please give them some custom on your return!

Depart NE on the A642, then turn right into Anstley Road immediately after the pelican crossing, signpost Allerton Bywater. Beyond the village a new road sweeps through the green, landscaped pitheaps. Then as you crest the rise you will see the first ings, possibly the draglines and the River Aire in the distance. When you reach Allerton Bywater turn right down past the Edward VII Working Men's Club and, 1.20 km (0.75 mile) later, turn left into Park Lane at the school opposite the pond. Traffic lights control your crossing of the A656, where you go straight ahead and follow signs for Fairburn Ings Nature Reserve which encompasses the biggest of the ponds.

Most of the ings are on your right, but there are a couple of ponds on the other side of the road, one heavily colonised by bull rushes and home to some of the shyer wildlife. It is worth a pause to peer quietly into the vegetation on the off chance of seeing something unusual. The wildfowl will eat out of your hand at the biggest ponds near Fairburn, but I liked the earlier smaller sheets of water, Newton Ings, where the birds floated about doing their own thing with the Ferrybridge towers in the distance.

On reaching Fairburn turn left into Gauk Road at the Wildgoose Gallery, then wiggle left and right over the little traffic-light controlled bridge which spans the A1(T) and head north towards South Milford. You slid into North Yorkshire just before reaching the biggest of the ings, but this is the bit that (to me) feels different, no hedges, sugar beet and electricity pylons. When you reach Lumby remember to keep left, it looks simple enough on the map but the roads are very narrow and what looks like a crossroads on the north side of the hamlet turns out to be nothing more than the exit from the farmyard!

Turn right into South Milford, then left at the first real opportunity and left again out of the village past the striking gatehouse at Steeton Hall. Take the next right at a hedgeless fork to the transmission mast to the E of Newthorpe. Turn left with the tarmac down past a brand new farm to the B1222 and head up a fair hill towards the A1 again. When you reach the thunderous Great North Road turn right up what amounts to a long slip road, then left , signposted Ledsham before joining the A1. The lanes seem like sanctuary after such proximity to the trunk road and the interlude through Ledsham and across to Kippax, although used by several folk as an access to the A1, is pleasant riding.

Keep left at the mini roundabout in Kippax, signposted Sports Centre, down the hill and bear right with the main road past the leisure facility, then at the bottom of the hill that takes you up to Great Preston you may notice Glencoe Terrace, and wonder how hard this climb is going to be. At the top of the hill turn right and up a bit more to Goody Cross where the left turn is signposted Little Preston, but you can see the blackened sandstone of Swillington Church and all that remains is to follow this road across to the A642, turn left and head down to the pub for some well earned refreshment.

One of the cycling elders of Ripponden sharing sweets near Blue Bell Road, Ripponden.

16

WY 16   RIPPONDEN RESERVOIRS

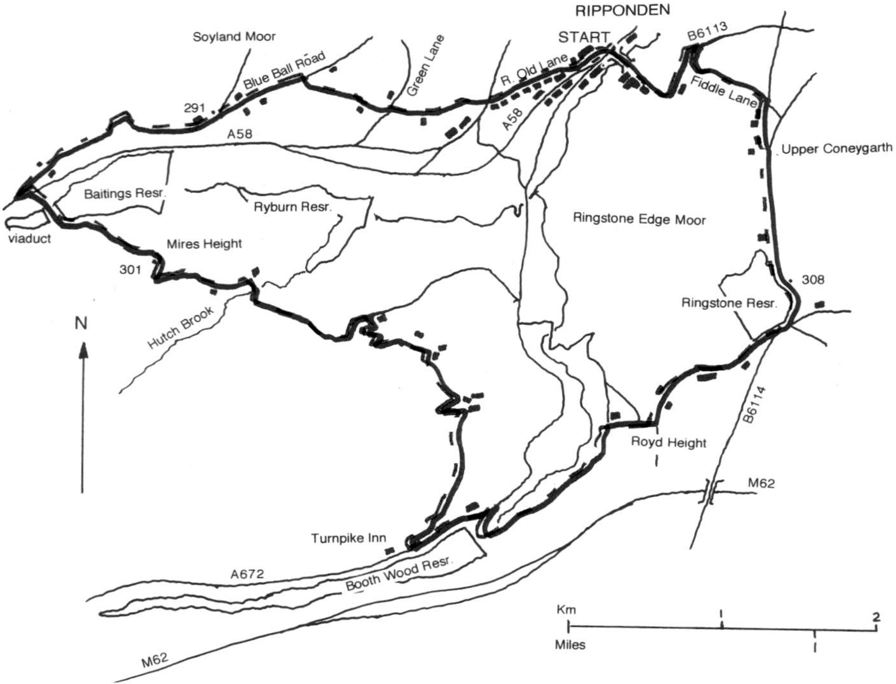

Upper Coneygarth

Fiddle Lane

B6113

RIPPONDEN

START

R. Ryburn

R. Old Lane

A58

308

Ringstone Edge Moor

Ringstone Resr.

B6114

M62

Royd Height

Green Lane

Soyland Moor

Blue Ball Road

A58

291

Baitings Resr.

Ryburn Resr

Mires Height

301

Hutch Brook

viaduct

Turnpike Inn

Booth Wood Resr

A672

M62

N

Km

Miles

2

16 RIPPONDEN RESERVOIRS

Total distance: 16.50 km (10.25 miles)
Grade: 5   Total climbing/downhilling: 381 m (1250 ft.)
High points: Blue Ball Road 291 m; Mires Height
                    301 m; Ringstone Edge Reservoir 308 m
Map: O S Landranger 110 Sheffield & Hudders-
                    field area
Facilities: Pubs in Ripponden, on the moor at Blue
                    Ball Road and by Baitings Reservoir, but
                    this is a wild moorland ride and in good
                    weather a high-level picnic will be well
                    rewarded

PLOTTING PLAN	App.	Map ref.	Dep.
START: Royd Lane carpark,			
off A58, Ripponden	-	110/040199	SW
Ripponden Old Lane	ENE	028194	W
Blue Ball Road, Soyland Moor	NE	018194	SW
A58, Baitings Reservoir, down			
over new bridge	NE	002188	SE
Pike Law junction, SP Pike End	W	024180	S
A672, Booth Wood Reservoir	NNE	027164	NE
Royd Height (not named			
on Landranger)	W	043172	NNE
B6114, Ringstone Edge Reservoir	S	051184	N
B6113, Ripponden Bank	SSE	045198	SW
FINISH: A58, Golden Fleece,			
Ripponden	SE	040198	-

You will enjoy this one! It was brilliant on a cold November day, so
it will be brilliant during the warmer months. It starts with a monumental

climb out of Ripponden, finishes with a wild and wacky downhill back to the town, and in between visits some really spectacular countryside. You can forget the history and the heritage for once, and just enjoy being out on the bike. I met one of the locals doing just that, but stopped to feed the horses with sweets high on the moor near Blue Ball Road, Most days since he retired, he gets the bike out and takes his time around the lanes, but on this occasion he was about to scuttle back down into Ripponden as huge, heavy clouds rolled over Soyland Moor from the west, threatening a down-pour which thankfully (for me) never materialised.

THE ROUTE
There is room for about 25 cars in the Royd Lane carpark, which is signposted P Free off the A58 north of the traffic lights in Ripponden. The ride really starts up Back Lane at the side of the Golden Fleece, so you will need to return to the A58, take one of your lowest gears and attack the hill. It is very steep initially, then flattens out for 150 metres, then climbs hard again when it bears right and becomes Ripponden Old Lane.

Well before the top of the hill one of the houses is called Falcon Manor. How appropriate — the view from the dining room window must be a splendid bird's eye view of the dale and across to Ringstone Edge Moor. I bet there's no rush to finish tea.

Straight ahead at the first crossroads and through the speed restriction signs. I had a wry smile to myself, now being allowed to go as fast as I liked, grinding up the hill at a mere 6 mph! Then high on the moor you come across Stones Cricket Club, on the only flat bit of land for miles around; but is it the highest cricket ground in the country? It must be one of the windiest. After cresting the rise beyond the Green Lane crossroads the gradient eases considerably, then it is T-junction left, and along between blackened, dry-stone walls, past the Blue Ball painted in the appropriate colour, still on single-track road, and gently down to the A58, Rochdale Road near Baitings Reservoir.

When you reach the main road, turn hairpin left, then right in 60 metres and down over the new Baitings Viaduct. The initial climb up the far side didn't seem too bad with a breeze at my back, but it does go on a bit. Then it is down the twisting road all the way to Hutch Brook, which feeds Ryburn Reservoir, and, inevitably up the far side. The downhill brought home to me the fact that *all* the houses up here have stone roofs, even the new ones; a nice bit of quality.

Turn right, uphill, signpost Pike End, which is the nose of the well-quarried ridge you can see to the south. About a third of the width of the single-track road up through the zigzags is stone sets, and they are on our side, so be prepared to use them if anything comes the other way — another instance when fat tyres will help. The road doesn't actually go over Pike End; it skirts the nose on a terraced road, some of which is quite a height, with a low Alpine-style wall. Not a place to loiter! This whole road is brilliant, hard work, but quietly unique.

Eventually you reach the A672 near the Turnpike Inn. Turn left, then look for the single-track lower dam road on the right in 0.61 km (0.38 mile). Single track, but well surfaced, it shoots down to the foot of Booth Wood dam then up the far side to crest the hill at the carpark. The downhill is bumpier, narrower and quite twisty — a Sunday motorist's nightmare, but you still meet them. Take care, they are probably right on their limit! Turn right with the main lane, steeply uphill to Royd Height, where you turn left at the T-junction at the top of a nasty little rise. This takes you along a typical, walled water board road all the way to Ringstone Edge Reservoir, actually a very pleasant ride in the latter stages.

Merge left onto the B6114 around the eastern side of Ringstone Reservoir and over the little rise at the old farm, the highest point on the ride, to start the final downhill, 2.93 ever-steepening kilometres

The M62 and Booth Wood Reservoir, west of Huddersfield, from the B6114 bridge.

(1.82 miles). Bear left at Upper Coneygarth, then left again into Fiddle Lane at Slack Farm, which can be a trifle muddy at times. Next steeply down to the main road in the shape of Ripponden Bank, where you turn hairpin left for the final flee to the Golden Fleece. By the time I arrived at the A58 even the Bolle Specials* hadn't prevented my eyes watering, absolutely brilliant!

* Protective glasses

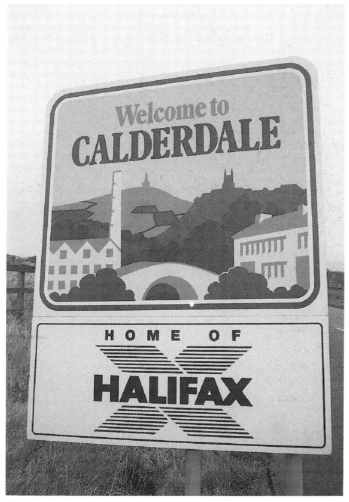

Guess who's the biggest employer in these parts ? Calderdale District
sign at the M62 bridge on the B6114.

WY 17   THE COLNE CLIMBER

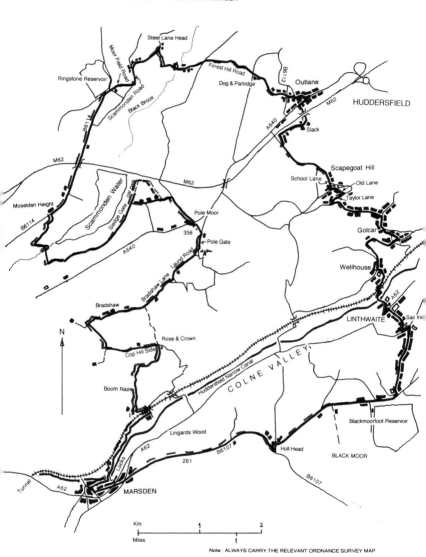

Km

Miles

Note : ALWAYS CARRY THE RELEVANT ORDNANCE SURVEY MAP

17 THE COLNE CLIMBER

Total distance:	32.06 km (19.91 miles)
Grade: 11	Total climbing/downhilling: 766 m (2513ft.)
High point:	Pole Moor, 358 m
Map:	O S Landranger 110 Sheffield & Huddersfield area
Facilities:	Food available in all the towns en route; snacks by the canal at Marsden.

PLOTTING PLAN	App.	Map ref.	Dep.
START: Wood Edge carpark, Scammonden Water B6114, Moselden Height.	-	110/055163	SSW
TR across M62	SSW	042160	NE
Steel Lane Head, down over Black Brook	SW	060186	S
Outlane, A640. Then first L under M62 in 300 m	W	084179	SW
Scapegoat Hill, L at TJ then R down Old Lane	NNW	088164	SE
Golcar, bear R down past School sign	WNW	097157	SE
A62, Linthwaite. TJTL then first R, steeply uphill!	N	097145	SE
Blackmoorfoot Reservoir. TJTR, SP Helme	N	099131	W
SH 261, B6107 above Lingards Wood	ENE	061121	SW
Marsden Locks	SW	052120	NNE
Booth Naze (not named on Landranger)	S	056133	N
Bradshaw	WSW	055145	E
Pole Moor, A640. Care, steep downhill approach	SE	066159	NW
FINISH: Scammonden Watercarpark	E	055162	-

Scammonden Water, W of Huddersfield, is the reservoir you can
see from the M62, where that incredibly high bridge carrying a minor
road crosses before you start the plunge down towards Manchester.
This ride starts above the reservoir next to the motorway, toddles
down to water level, climbs, in a most unreasonable fashion, up to
that minor road which turns out to be the B6114, then crosses that
high level bridge, and the pattern for the ride is set!

This is the hardest ride in the book, probably best left until last,
although the opposite school of thought might recommend doing it
first, then everything else is easy by comparison! It is as much an
industrial archeology tour as a bike ride — reflections of Colne
valley's mighty industrial past, with mills and the Huddersfield
Narrow Canal at its most spectacular in Marsden. You will cross
the flight of locks and can do a 300 metre diversion to the end of
the Standedge Tunnel, which is signposted in Marsden — the longest tunnel, at the highest point of any artificial waterway in Britain. It
was built to Imperial standards so it seems right that those meas-
urements come first : 5,698 yards (5.21 km) long, at a height of 637
feet (194 m), finished in 1811.

There are totally rural moments too. The mean Bradshaw loop
runs through a collection of exposed hill farms where once every
enclosure was thick with sheep. This is dramatic countryside where
you need not only a fair dose of Yorkshire grit, but possibly a few
rock pitons for the harder climbs!

THE ROUTE
Scammonden Dam is signposted off the A640 at Pole Moor, W of
Huddersfield.

Turn right out of the Wood Edge carpark, straight ahead into
Sledge Gate and make for the head of the reservoir, past the
entrance to the sailing club, where it seems that there are always
wind-eddies whistling around the corrie and down to the water.

S bends at the bottom of the hill will drop your speed, so the steep, bumpy, unrelenting climb starts from a virtual standstill. Cruel! Take care over the angled drains on the hill, which raise the standard of this bumpy single-track road from difficult to near horrendous!

When you reach the B6114 at Moselden Height turn right, avoiding the chained dogs, and ride across the bridge over the M62, heeding the wind warning! A little coal house at the side of a building opposite the quarry has some of the biggest roofing slabs in the county, but they are surpassed later. Ringstone Reservoir appears as you crest the rise, which is where you turn right into Moor Field Road, signposted Krumlin. Bear left with Scammonden Road at a sort of T-junction, then right 50 metres beyond the telephone kiosk, downhill into a narrow single-track road. This takes you to Steel Lane Head where you turn hairpin right, down the exciting Steel Lane to the mill chimney. No doubt you have encountered stone sets on corners before, but this lot develop into the full road width. Steady down to the bridge!

Cross the bridge at Black Brook — obviously once part of the mill yard — then it is up, up, and bear right uphill into Forest Hill Road. On a cold December day this was a bleak climb fringed with black heather, but at the height of summer the vista should be a whole lot better. Give Way at the Dog & Partridge, but straight on with Forest Hill Road, then down at last past the New Inn to Outlane, turning right onto the B6112 for a short way to the main road.

The A640 is a lot quieter these days, so turn right near the Waggon & Horses, then left in 300 metres at the old toilets to go under the M62 to Slack. The road is very narrow through Slack, then left up to Scapegoat Hill which is a tougher climb than it looks. On the crest of the hill go straight ahead into School Lane, down past the school itself, then left at the T-junction and immediately right into the skinny Old Lane, which in turn takes you down to a very minor crossroads with Taylor Lane at Valley View. Turn right down Taylor

Lane, hairpin left at the end, then downhill past The Commercial all the way to Golcar.

In Golcar turn right with the main road at the chemists, then look to fork right into a narrow downhill guarded by a School sign at Cliffe Ashe. Follow this road down all the way to the Brook Lane crossroads, where you turn right, downhill again, around past Drake Fibres, then uphill into Wellhouse. Look to turn left, downhill into Lowestwood Lane near the school and follow this down, under the railway then across the Huddersfield Narrow Canal and up to the A62 at Linthwaite.

Turn left at the A62, then first right up Hoyle Ing through the factory. Get a low gear before you turn in, because it is seriously steep and sustained. Near the top of the hill, you will be confronted by the pig beaming down at you from the Sair Inn, which brews its own beer — a great temptation! A hundred metres after the pub you reach the main high road through Linthwaite Turn left uphill, then first right past the telephone kiosk for a few hundred metres of relief.

The horizontal skyline of the vast dam wall greets you at Blackmoorfoot, where you turn right, signposted Helme, then head due W all the way to Holt Head. Turn left at the T-junction at Holt Head, signpost Marsden, then right in 100 metres onto the B6107, again signposted Marsden, up past the White House Hotel then down all the way to Marsden, crossing the A62 again in the process.

Brougham Road takes you into the centre of Marsden, where you turn right at the main street, then T-junction right again, unless you wish to visit the end of the Standedge Tunnel. Stop at the canal in any case, for there is a fascinating flight of locks, and the little shop with the green shed does sandwiches. The road along to the railway bridge undulates, affording great views of the canal reservoirs and their wildlife. Then it is sharp left immediately under the railway, into a very narrow road up the N side of the bridge abutment and into the Bradshaw loop.

It might look a bit complicated on the map, but all you do is follow the skinny tarmac, up, up and a bit more up. There are great views back down the Colne valley, before you are thrust into the moors again — windy, bleak and heartbreaking in a strong westerly! Follow the tarmac to the Rose & Crown crossroads, where you turn left up Cop Hill Side, after which it is T-junction turn right at a farm junction, same again at another, then keep left with Bradshaw Lane, which becomes Laund Road as you head for the transmission masts.

Eventually you come to a T-junction with Pole Gate. Turn left uphill again, then left again after 200 metres, pass a tiny road on the left, over the crest — the highest point on the route — and down to the A640 at Pole Moor. Give Way at the main road, turn hairpin right then immediately hairpin left, signposted Scammonden Dam, possibly the way you came, and follow downhill to the carpark. There is a final sting in the tail, if you are totally dedicated. Go straight on at the bend at the bottom of the hill and up the narrow road past the farms to the carpark, but the longer lower route is a lot easier. Whichever you choose, you deserve a medal!

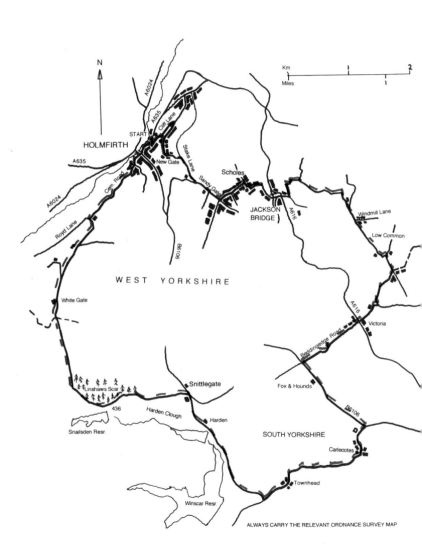

ALWAYS CARRY THE RELEVANT ORDNANCE SURVEY MAP

18 HOLMFIRTH & SNITTLEGATE

Total distance:	21.88 km (13.59 miles)
Grade: 8	Total climbing/downhilling: 536 m (1759 ft)
High point:	Linshaws Scar, near Snailsden Reservoir, Harden Clough, 436 m
Map:	O S Landranger 110 Sheffield & Huddersfield area
Facilities:	Full range of eating establishments in Holmfirth, five pubs en route.

PLOTTING PLAN	App.	Map ref.	Dep.
START: Station Road car park (A635), Holmfirth	-	110/144083	SW
Cemetery Road, Holmfirth	NE	139076	SW
White Gate	N	128057	SSE
Snittlegate crossroads	W	150043	SSE
Townhead	SW	164028	NE
Fox & Hounds, B6106	SE	171044	NW
Victoria crossroads, A616	SW	178054	NE
Low Common, single-track road	SE	179068	NW
South View/A616, Jackson Bdge	E	166074	W
Sandy Gate crossroads, Scholes	NE	156074	NW
Cliff Lane, Holmfirth. Hairpin left, downhill!	SW	148086	WSW
FINISH: Station Road (A635), Holmfirth	NE	144083	-

This route is tough. Perhaps because nearly all the climbing is done from the start, 301 metres from Holmfirth to Linshaws Scar, in one fell swoop. Of course you get it all back, the final precipitous downhill lying within the confines of Holmfirth itself — quite an end to the ride!

Even strangers to the area will have heard of Holme Moss, site of one of the first British television transmitters, providing coverage for the whole of the north of England. So you can imagine the terrain that surrounds the Holme valley.

The ride slips into South Yorkshire past Winscar Reservoir and the end of the famous Woodhead railway tunnel. Though sadly closed to rail traffic the tunnel is still functioning, amazingly, as a trans-Pennine arm of the Central Electricity Generating Board's national grid, eliminating the necessity for a line of pylons across these wild and magnificent heights.

If you are not acquainted with Holmfirth you will be impressed with the steepness of the valley sides, even by West Yorkshire standards, and little surprised to learn that there have been several disastrous floods, but the contrast between the warmth of the town and the wildness of the surrounding moors is absolute. This is a wild tour, even on the best of days.

THE ROUTE

You will find the Station Road long stay carpark on the A635, on the E side of the river, signposted Wakefield. There are only about 20 spaces but there is usually a vacant bay or two. If this is full, use the main town carpark on the A6024 and adjust the ride accordingly.

Set off downhill to the main crossroads on the E side of the river. Then go straight ahead where the A635 bends right, and jink left, steeply uphill into a narrow road which usually has a line of parked cars along one side. Climb steeply, then fork right into Cemetery Road and up past (surprise, surprise) the cemetery. The gradient eases after the graveyard, but still climbs relentlessly to the T-junction at Royd Lane.

Turn left into Royd Lane, which soon swings right, then find a rhythm which will take you all the way up to Linshaws Scar, near

Snailsden Reservoir, the highest point on the route. There is a short respite near White Gate Farm, but it's a slog all the way apart from that.

Eventually you reach Snittlegate crossroads, where you turn right to be welcomed to Barnsley! It might have been the dour day, but these open expanses seemed to be moors with a vengeance, and Harden Farm just over the crest seemed to be putting a very brave face on it — guardian of Snailsden and the reservoirs. Above the road at Winscar Reservoir a kestrel was hanging, virtually motionless in a wave of wind, cocking his head at me like a clockwork toy as if to say hurry up and get past, but I was enjoying the downhill and only interrupted the hunt for a few seconds.

Turn left, signposted Thurlstone at the next T-junction, down through Townhead and along to the B6106 beyond Carlecotes. Here you turn left, uphill past the Fox & Hounds, the dog on the pub sign having a very knowing look about him — a great bit of artwork. Turn right at the crossroads beyond the pub at the top of the hill, into Beddingedge Road, then straight ahead at Victoria when you reach the A616, then wiggle left uphill, over the crest and left towards Low Common.

There is a triangular junction on Low Common, where the main road swings right, but we use the rough left-hand side of the triangle, turning left then immediately right onto a single-track road up towards the farm — the road was very muddy at the farm. This bids farewell to South Yorkshire. Next straight on past Windmill Lane to fork left at the next house and down a steep, twisting, single track-road towards Jackson Bridge. The distance from the triangle to the turn into South View, Jackson Bridge is 2.60 km (1.62 miles). Look out for it, it is easy to miss, but you will soon realise your mistake - the road starts to climb again. (You will guess that I overshot!)

South View takes you down to the A616, where you go straight ahead, then steeply down to the bridge itself, where it is straight

Harden Farm above Winscar Reservoir, Snailsden. Remote, open
to the elements and overlooking a bleak moor.

ahead again and past the White Horse, which devotees of *Last of
the Summer Wine* will recognise immediately, even without the
advert for 'Grandma Batty's Traditional Yorkshire Pudding'. From
here it is uphill again, weaving through Scholes. Keep left with Paris
Rd at the Boot & Shoe, then turn R into Sandy Gate at the 40 mph signs.

After only 450 metres (0.28 mile) of Sandy Gate, fork right into
Stake Lane — the upper road — then turn left, downhill at a precipitous little triangle marked by a white end to the retaining wall.
This twisty lane takes you down through New Gate, which isn't
named on the Landranger, up the final slight rise to the junction
with the aptly named Cliff Lane, which you will see heralded by a
blue sign Unsuitable for vehicles over 6'6" wide, which could also
apply to the length!

This is the final downhill. Narrow, fairly twisty, precipitous (which
seems to have become the word for this ride!) and culminating in a
tight hairpin right down to Station Road, and an even tighter left
onto the A635 to finish. Take care, these final turns are really tight.

Some of Tetley, Brewery's older transport , normally pulled by a horse,
but today ...

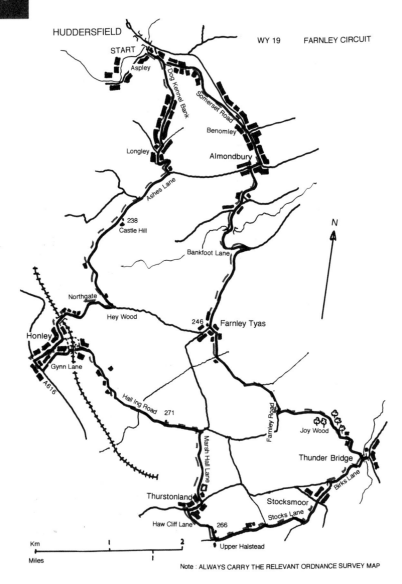

19

HUDDERSFIELD

WY 19   FARNLEY CIRCUIT

START

Aspley

Dog Kennel Bank

Somerset Road

Benomley

Longley

Almondbury

Ashes Lane

238
Castle Hill

Bankfoot Lane

N

Northgate

Hey Wood

246   Farnley Tyas

Honley

Gynn Lane

A616

Hall Ing Road   271

Farnley Road

Joy Wood

Thunder Bridge

Marsh Hall Lane

Birks Lane

Thurstonland

Stocksmoor

Stocks Lane

Haw Cliff Lane   266

Km   1   2

Miles

Upper Halstead

Note : ALWAYS CARRY THE RELEVANT ORDNANCE SURVEY MAP

19 FARNLEY CIRCUIT

Total distance:	21.64 km (13.44 miles)
Grade: 8	Total climbing/downhilling: 560 m (1837 ft.)
High points:	Castle Hill, 238 m; Hall Ing Road, 271m
	Upper Halstead, 266 m; Farnley Tyas, 246m
Map:	O S Landranger 110 Sheffield & Huddersfield area
Facilities:	Everything you could wish in Huddersfield ! Several pubs on the ride route.

PLOTTING PLAN	App.	Map ref.	Dep.
START: Maple Street, Aspley, Huddersfield	-	110/152162	ESE
Hall Cross Road, Longley	N	155151	SSW
Castle Hill	NE	151141	SW
Northgate, Hey Wood	NW	151129	W
A616 / Gynn Lane, Newtown	NW	143119	NE
Hall Ing Road	W	162115	E
Haw Cliff Lane, Thurstonland	NE	165104	SSE
Fulstone Road, Stocksmoor	W	181105	NE
Thunder Bridge	SSW	188114	WNW
Golden Cock, Farnley Tyas	SE	165128	N
Almondbury	SSE	167149	ENE
Somerset Road, Benomley	SE	162157	NW
FINISH: Maple Street, Aspley, Huddersfield	ESE	152162	-

There are few cities in England where you can start a really testing bike ride from the riverside, include in excess of 1,800 feet of downhilling and of course the climbs that go with it, return virtually to the city centre, and cram it all into just over 20 kilometres (13 miles).

You can at Huddersfield, and also throw in a selection of single-track lanes, a couple of which are exciting to say the least! This is the Farnley circuit.

Huddersfield itself is still an important cloth making, weaving and tailoring centre, and when you ride the steep-sided surrounding hills you will realise how a city of this size grew up here. In the days of water power, there must have been plenty generated by the rivers and streams tumbling down from the surrounding fells. It must be one of the hilliest cities in the country, with few places flat enough for a football pitch, a regular source of complaint from visiting teams in the lower leagues, usually countered by the locals saying "Show us somewhere flatter!"

The first destination of the ride is Castle Hill, topped by the Victoria Tower and the Castle Hill Hotel endowed with views close to Alpine proportions, although the initial climb of 173 metres (568 ft) from the riverside might ensure few cyclists among the customers! The ancient Brigantes, under their queen Cartimandua, had what must have been an impressive vitrified fort here in the first century AD. Although mainly found in Scotland or France, vitrified forts had glazed walls where the stone, rich in silica, had been vitrified by fire. Whether intentionally or by accident is the subject of much learned debate. As you might expect, the Brigantes were followed by the Romans and the Normans.

Thunder Bridge is the distant turning point of the ride, but if you are expecting, as I was, a boiling chasm rumbling far beneath an ancient bridge, you will be disappointed. I failed to source the heritage of the impressive name, but it's a bonny little place nevertheless.

The final climb takes you up to Almondbury, now virtually a suburb of Huddersfield, pronounced Ainsbury by the locals. Here there is a Tudor house at the T-junction near the Woolpack, used by the local Conservative Association, and a grammar school founded in

1608 under a charter granted by James 1.Then it is down, down, down all the way back to Huddersfield.

THE ROUTE

There is usually room to park in the street along the riverside, at the rough carpark in Maple Street or in Maple Street itself.

Depart ESE along Maple Street, right into Somerset Road at the one-way triangle at the top, then right into the wide Dog Kennel Bank and up the hill past the entrance to the school. Stick with the never-ending hill all the way to Longley, turning right at the end of Hall Cross Road, opposite the Longley Fisheries (chippy), then bear left and steeply uphill into Longley Lane. The tight hairpins will take you up to the T-junction with Ashes Lane to conclude one of the hardest 1.80 km (1.12 miles) in this guide.

Turn right into Ashes Lane and around to Castle Hill, the road providing a terrific sheep's eye view of Huddersfield and the valley. Once over the crest near the Castle Hill Hotel, the road drops in a series of undulations, then climbs a little more to Hey Wood, which you reach after 2.29 km (1.42 miles). Turn hairpin right into Northgate, signpost Honley, then down all the way to the A616, but there is a skiver's alternative which always appeals to me if I can cut out a bit of climbing!

If you don't mind a bit of uneven track, you can turn left up to Honley railway station, which is well signposted, and then either nip through the tunnel under the line which will bring you out after a short walk on the E side of the track in a new housing estate, or stick with the rough track along the W side of the line and turn left through the railway arch when you reach Gynn Lane.

Genuine riders! will go all the way down to the A616, turn left, then left again into Gynn Lane which takes you up under the railway, then climbs relentlessly all the way to the crossroads in Hall Ing Road.

I pulled over and stopped when a 4WD Nissan Patrol caught me as I toiled up the ever narrowing lane, more out of fear than courtesy when I heard it spinning wheels on the wet tarmac at the nasty little bend on Longley Hill, but felt safe after it had passed because it filled the road, and surely nothing would now come hurtling down towards me!

Hall Ing Road continues beyond the crossroads high on the hill, then it is right and downhill into Marsh Hall Lane which takes you to Thurstonland. When you reach the T-junction in Thurstonland turn right, signpost New Mill, then left into the very narrow Haw Cliff Lane, past the Post Office and over the hill to Upper Halstead. Here you turn left into the narrow, potholed Halstead Lane towards Stocksmoor. Keep right into Stocks Lane, down through the farm, then T-junction left into Fulstone Road, through Stocksmoor itself, then right down Birks Lane to Thunder Bridge. There were a lot of leaves on the steepest part of the hill which added to the excitement. I suspect a frosty day could induce similar conditions. Take care.

Turn left before the bridge into Grange Lane and up the hill to Joy Wood — the mind boggles — a spectacular beechwood, then T-junction right into Farnley Road in the midst of open countryside. Keep left with the main road to Farnley Tyas, then turn right at the Golden Cock when you get there. The tight turn into Bankfoot Lane is 1.11 km (0.69 mile) from the Tyas turn, watch for it, you could well overshoot.

Down over Bank Foot Bridge, then up the last climb through Almondbury Common, past the mill, on to Almondbury where you turn right, down past the Radcliffe Arms, the Woolpack and the Tudor house to the T-junction. Here you turn left along the main street with its huge speed humps, then slightly left into Somerset Road and back down, down, down to Huddersfield. Grade 8 cracked, well done!

Mallards at Cannon Hall Country Park, November.

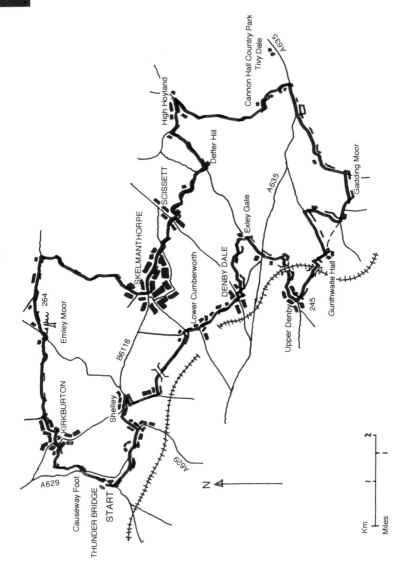

Cannon Hall Country Park
Tivy Dale
A635

High Hoyland

Deffer Hill

A635

SCISSETT

Gadding Moor

SKELMANTHORPE

Exley Gate

Emley Moor

264

Lower Cumberworth

DENBY DALE

B6116

Upper Denby

245

Gunthwaite Hall

KIRKBURTON

Shelley

A629

Causeway Foot
THUNDER BRIDGE
START

A629

N

Km
Miles

20 EMLEY MOOR

Total distance:	35.19 km (21.86 miles)
Grade: 10	Total climbing/downhilling: 679 m (2228 ft.)
High point:	Upper Denby, 245 m; Emley Moor, 264 m
Map:	O S Landranger 110 Sheffield & Huddersfield area
Facilities:	Woodman Inn & Restaurant at Thunder Bridge, many pubs on the route, & who knows, you may even descend into Denby Dale at the time of one of the great pies.

PLOTTING PLAN	App.	Map ref.	Dep.
START: Quarry carpark, Thunder Bridge	-	110/189116	SSW
Zebra crossing A629, signpost Shelley	WNW	200108	NNE
B6116 Shelley, down Near Bank	W	207111	SW
Lower Cumberworth	NNW	224092	SE
Denby Dale, bear L into Cuckstool Road	W	232085	ENE
Exley Gate	NE	241082	SW
Gunthwaite Hall Farm, stick with tarmac	NNW	238066	NE
Gadding Moor	WSW	256061	NNE
A635, Tivy Dale, signpost Cannon Hall	WSW	276074	NNW
High Hoyland	SE	266100	SW
Wheatley Hill Farm	S	252097	N
B6116 Skelmanthorpe	SE	238104	NW
Jagger Lane, Emley	SSW	238130	W
TV mast, Emley Moor, right into Jagger Lane (again!)	NE	220130	W
Kirkburton, down to cross B6116, then A629	NE	201129	SW
FINISH: Quarry carpark, Thunder Bridge	NNE	189116	-

It wasn't intentional, but unsurprisingly the tour that visits the Emley Moor TV mast is one of the hardest in terms of total climbing, although the overall height achieved isn't the greatest. The mast is the most obvious feature on the skyline in Kirklees and a fitting climax to any ride in these parts, or perhaps the source of great relief knowing that the rest of the route is downhill once you reach it!

The route uses mainly minor roads in the triangle created by the A629, A635 and A637, but sneaks south across the border into South Yorkshire via Gunthwaite Hall to Cannon Hall Country Park. This is well worth a visit and an ideal place for a halfway picnic if you are prepared to share it with moorhen, mallard, coot, Muscovy ducks, Canada geese and the occasional swan — mute I think, on the winter day I was there.

En route, you ride through the famous pie village of Denby Dale. There is no pattern to the baking of these great pies, and I mean great — the 1964 delicacy, baked to raise the money to build a new village hall, weighed 6 tons. The tradition started in 1788 to commemorate the recovery of George III from 'mental affliction', but there is no record of whose mad idea it was to bake a giant pie. There have been pies to celebrate Waterloo in 1846, others in 1896 and 1928, but the most infamous was the Great Jubilee Pie of 1887 which went bad and was hastily buried! Normally, as you will find, Denby Dale is an ordered place with the inhabitants going about their usual business, but beware the days when pie fever hits town — the whole of Yorkshire descends upon the place.

THE ROUTE
There is space for about twenty cars in the old quarry at the north end of Thunder Bridge.

Depart SSW through Thunder Bridge, past the Woodman, then left up to the A629. Turn right when you reach the main road, then left immediately after the Zebra crossing, signpost Shelley, 1.55 km

(0.96 mile) after starting. The up and down to Shelley, then across to Lower Cumberworth, gets you off the main road as soon as possible, and gets you pretty warm too.

Merge right onto the B6116 at Shelley, then hairpin right into the steep downhill of Near Bank within 300 metres. This shoots you down past dale bottom factories then left into Long Moor Lane and around under the old railway bridge and steeply up again towards Lower Cumberworth, which is one of the highest points on the ride!

When you reach the T-junction at Shelley Woodhouse Lane, turn R, past a road on the left, then bear left at the Foresters, signposted Denby Dale, up through Lower Cumberworth and down to the pie village, noting the fine railway viaduct en route.

Turn left onto the A636 in Denby Dale, then immediately right before the Corner Shop into Miller Lane. Cross the bridge, up the hill, then left into Cuckstool Lane, which drops initially then becomes narrower as it swings right up to Exley Gate. Keep going right and you can't go wrong. Straight across the A635, pausing momentarily, then up to Upper Denby, where you realise you must have blinked and missed Lower Denby. Turn left into Gunthwaite Lane after you pass The George and watch out for the potholes. The railway bridge has become a gentle zigzag, then turn left with the tarmac into the very narrow Coach Gate Lane when you get to Gunthwaite Hall Farm. Unless you really love mud I don't think you will be tempted by Gunthwaite Lane!

The ride uses the next road on the right, Broad Oak Lane, fringed, correctly with oak trees, a nice bit of Yorkshire style. Then it is T-junction left at the pond, straight on past a road on the right and up the hill controlled by a very mossy sign announcing a weight restriction of 3 tons. This takes you to Gadding Moor, where you turn left down to the A635, joining it at the works of Naylor Clayware at a slightly complicated junction, but basically you turn right along towards Tivy Dale until you reach the brown signpost for Cannon Hall.

Even if you aren't having a picnic you must nip in to Cannon Hall Country Park for five minutes with the wildfowl, then it is up over the top and up again to High Hoyland, where you turn hairpin left, signposted West Clayton, then left again downhill into Hollin House Lane and back into West Yorkshire. The undulating lane, blocked on the day by an apparently lost timber lorry, climbs up to Deffer Hill where you turn right, downhill, into Wheatley Hill Lane, then down all the way to Scissett.

Straight across the A636 into Highbridge Lane, steadily up to The Windmill at the junction with the B6116, then straight through Skelmanthorpe as far as Station Road at the far end of town. Here the signpost for Emley had been flattened against the wall. Turn right into Station Road, down past the terminus of the Kirklees Light Railway, past the old colliery, then up, up, towards Emley.

On reaching the T-junction at Jagger Lane, west of Emley, turn left, uphill for the final pull to the mast. Absolutely horrendous in a westerly wind; just awful at all other times! The transmission mast turns out to be a stark bit of architecture, but impressive nevertheless, surrounded by a gaggle of lesser metal versions. Now turn right , surprisingly, into Jagger Lane again, looking virtually due W to Castle Hill above Huddersfield (Route 19).

The final downhill starts here, down to Kirkburton where you bear left with the main road at The Junction, jink right and left across the B6116 at the Royal. Next across the A629 at Causeway Foot into Thunderbridge Lane, and lastly down to the quarry. I suppose I enjoyed it! I hope you do.

Newmillerdam and the country park lake, November afternoon.

21

WY 21   WOOLLEY & WINTERSETT

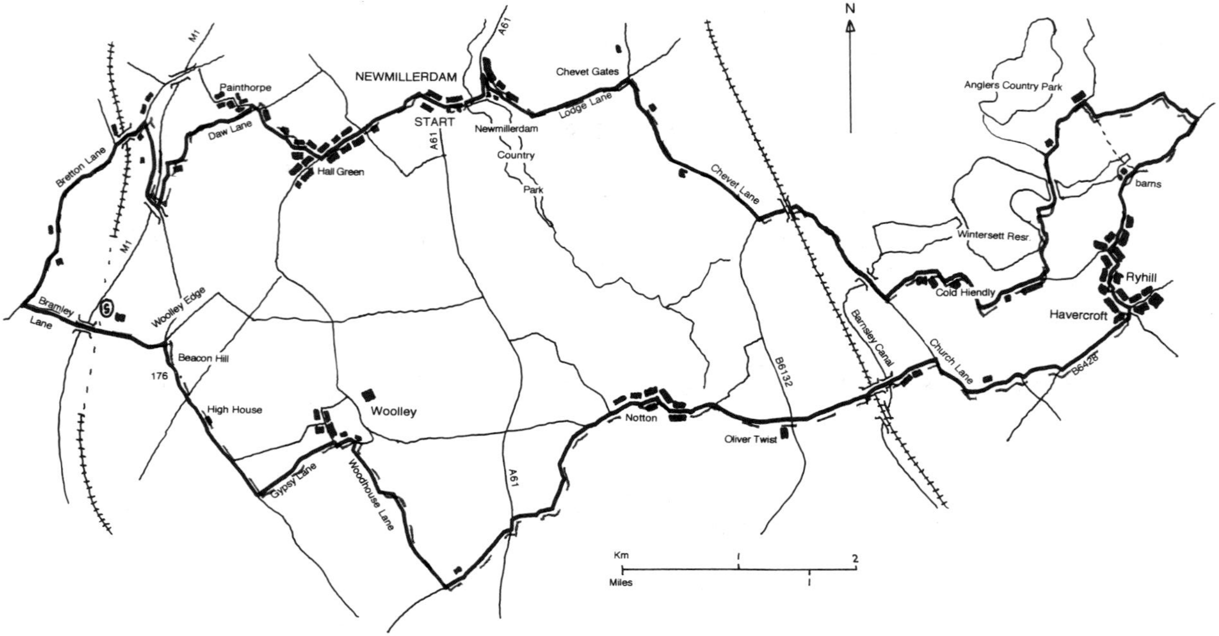

N

Km

Miles

Anglers Country Park

Wintersett Resr

barns

Ryhill

Havercroft

Cold Hiendly

Church Lane

B6134

Barnsley Canal

B6132

Oliver Twist

Notton

Chevet Lane

A61

Chevet Gates

Lodge Lane

Newmillerdam Country Park

A61

A61

NEWMILLERDAM

START

Woolley

Woodhouse Lane

Hall Green

Painthorpe

Dew Lane

Bramley Lane

Woodhouse Lane

Upton Lane

High House

Beacon Hill

Woolley Edge

176

M1

Bramley Lane

Benton Lane

M1

Note ALWAYS CARRY THE RELEVANT ORDNANCE SURVEY MAP

WOOLLEY & WINTERSETT

Total distance:	31.86 km (19.79 miles)
Grade: 5	Total climbing/downhilling: 351 m (1152 ft.)
High point:	Woolley Edge 176 m
Map:	O S Landranger 110 Sheffield & Huddersfield area
Facilities:	Fox & Hounds and Beuley Cafe at Newmillerdam, several pubs en route including the Oliver Twist at the B6132 crossroads near Notton.

PLOTTING PLAN	App.	Map ref.	Dep.
START: Main carpark, Newmillerdam	-	110/331157	NW
Hall Green, TR past Community Centre	NE	319153	NW
Daw Lane, Painthorpe, aim to cross M1	NE	307155	S
Bretton Lane, sustained climb	N	297148	S
Woolley Edge Xroads, 175m	SW	305136	SSE
Gypsy Lane, Woolley single-track tarmac	SW	317126	NE
A61, Barnsley Road T-junction turn left then right	SW	335121	ENE
B6132, Oliver Twist crossroads near Notton	W	359130	ENE
B6428, signpost Havercroft (SH 66 Ryhill, roughstuff	W	381134	NE
option, turn left at the barns	SW	388152	NW
Back Lane, turn L past the pond	SW	393156	NW
Wintersett Reservoir	N	381150	S
Cold Hiendley T-junction	NE	367141	NW
Chevet Gates Xroads, B6132	SSE	345160	WSW
FINISH: Newmillerdam	ENE	331157	-

Newmillerdam, at the start, is an entertainment in itself. Still within the city boundary of Wakefield, it is a brilliant little lake with an abundance of water fowl which makes it worth a visit at any time of year.

Woolley Edge to most will mean a service area on the M1, but the older and more permanent reality is its spectacular setting with a steep approach to the curving ridge, affording impressive views to the N and W. Needless to say the climb demands a lot of effort, but is well worth it.

Between Notton and Ryhill you will cross a double bridge spanning both the railway and a canal. Little now remains of the Barnsley Canal, opened in 1799, which ran for 24 km (15 miles) from Wakefield to Barnsley. Its principal purpose was to exploit the extensive coalfield in the area. You cross it twice. It closed in 1953.

Wintersett Reservoir is a fine sheet of water, rich in life at any time, but to be there, cresting the rise after the first crossing of the north-eastern arm as the sun was setting can only be described as stunning. If only I had remembered to put lights on the bike I would have sat there, probably freezing, until it disappeared. As it was I dawdled around the edge, supposed to be making progress, until the road veered away from the water, then beetled back to Newmillerdam before darkness overtook me. But I'll be back.

THE ROUTE

Turn right out of the main carpark entrance (or sneak out of the bottom corner) then turn immediate left past the Fox & Hounds carpark into School Hill. Next up over the top where it becomes Boyne Hill as you swing left, through the offset crossroads near the Bay Horse and into Hall Green. Turn right, before Ashworths, past the Community Centre, and Crigglestone Sports Club, then look to turn left into Daw Lane as soon as you reach Painthorpe. This takes you past the rugby fields, down to the bottom of the motorway embankment, then up to the traffic lights where you turn right over the M1.

Turn left at the next T-junction, past the old Station Hotel, looking a bit forlorn down in the hole, over the railway and left with the main road, Bretton Lane, into a steep and sustained climb, the first half of the ascent to Woolley Edge. Before you reach West Bretton turn left into Bramley Lane — a bit of a 'breather' — cross the motorway again then straight up to the crossroads on Beacon Hill, the highest part of Woolley Edge, 176 m. Turn right, signpost Woolley. The view is most impressive, even peering through approaching showers!

It is now mostly down, although there is a slight climb at High House Farm, but this is easily overcome with a bout of overgeared effort. Then it is straight past the first turn to Woolley village, but left into Gypsy Lane with its roadside nature reserve, then turn right into Back Lane, around the corner and right again into Woodhouse Lane. This will take you through the fields to another T-junction where you turn left down to the A61, Barnsley Road.

Take care at the A61. You want to turn left, then right in 100 metres into another single track-road to Notton. When you get to Notton turn right, through the village and down to the B6132 at the Oliver Twist. Follow the brown Anglers Country Park signpost straight ahead, then over the double bridge across the railway and the Barnsley Canal, and down to the T-junction where you turn right into Church Lane.

Now head for Havercroft, jinking left where the map makes it look as if you should go straight on, then left again when you reach the B6428. Turn left when you reach Havercroft, past the tiny, red bus shelter and follow the signs for Nostell into Nostell Lane, which would eventually take you to the priory but we turn off well before. On the north side of Ryhill an opportunity arises for a bit of roughstuff, if you are so inclined. Turn left at the barns in the dip into a grassy track signposted Bridleway and follow this NNW to Wintersett. You will see that the map shows it cutting through an arm of the reservoir, so be prepared for a bit of a splash at most times of the year! The road route turns left into another Back Lane opposite a bus stop, and past a little pond.

Turn left again at the Wintersett T-junction, past the Anglers Retreat, past the road to the Anglers Country Park, then around the east side of Wintersett Reservoir. When you reach the junction at the top of the rise, turn right to Cold Hiendley, right again at the T-junction, then eventually under the railway bridge to the B6132, where it is right again into Chevet Lane, signpost Sandal.

This heralds the final climb of the day — a steady pull up, then a quick downhill approach to the Chevet Gates crossroads where you want to turn left into Lodge Lane and Newmillerdam Country Park. Take care on the fringes of Newmillerdam, as the road is very narrow. Turn left at the A61, down past the Dam Inn to finish.